FROM THE
TOP
TURRET

A Memoir of World War II

and the American Dream

GERARD J. CAPORASO
with MARY V. DANIELSEN

FROM THE TOP TURRET

A Memoir of World War II
and the American Dream

GERARD J. CAPORASO
with **MARY V. DANIELSEN**

Copyright © 2014 Gerard J. Caporaso
All rights reserved.

ISBN: 0615696325
ISBN 13: 9780615696324

Library of Congress Control Number: 2012949055
Documented Legacy, LLC
Mount Laurel NJ

To my wife,

Virginia Stanek Caporaso,

and my sons,

James, Steven and Robert Caporaso

ACKNOWLEDGEMENTS

This memoir would not have been possible without the cumulative efforts of many people who helped make this project a reality. What started out as a willingness to sit down and talk about my military experience in World War II and my remembrances as a prisoner of war evolved to more than 20 hours of audio interviews, a day-long tour of restored B-17s and a reunion with my crew pilot's daughter. I remembered things that I had long forgotten. It was as if I had cracked open the door to the over-stuffed attic and finally picked through all the valuables I stored decades ago.

It's not easy remembering exact details nearly 70 years later. Some stories I can retell as if they happened yesterday while others had to be nudged out of hiding. Still, there are some stories that I'd just assume forget, rather than leave unpleasant reminders of myself behind. I never thought I had enough of a story to warrant a printed book. This was the easiest way to share my story with the next generations in my extended family.

With my deepest gratitude I would like to thank the following people and organizations:

To my family for encouraging me over the years to tell my story. Every life has a story. It's my hope that this memoir encourages each of you to write your own. To my sons, Bobby, Steve, and Jimmy, for making me do this project. At first, I just agreed to talk to someone. It didn't take long before I looked forward to my interview and writing sessions with Mary Danielsen. I almost didn't want the project to end.

To Brigid O'Donnell, daughter of my pilot Lt. Raymond Bye, for sharing an instant friendship and helping us to illustrate Crew K90's missions overseas, especially on the toughest day of our lives together. She flew to New Jersey during a terrible snow storm to meet with me and graciously shared her archives of World War II photos, some of which took years of research and online snooping to acquire. She graciously agreed to share several key photos with us for the writing of this project. I will forever be in debited to her.

To Fred Greyer of The Possum Escape Line for connecting me to Brigid O'Donnell.

To the researchers and web masters at the Eighth Air Force Museum, the National World War II Museum, Air Force Historical Research Agency, the 96th Bomb Group Association, the 100th Bomb Group Foundation, and the forum posters on the Army Air Forces website for all their help and guidance. To the National Archives, Ancestry.com and Wikipedia.com for making so much information publicly available.

To the members of the Second Schweinfurt Mission Association for sharing their family photos and military records that helped jog my memory. It is my wish that the great people of both nations shall forever remain friends and the history of Black Thursday is never forgotten.

To the Collings Foundation of Stow, Mass for making me feel like a celebrity during a tour of restored B-17s at both the Monmouth Executive Airport and the Morristown Airport in New Jersey. Sitting on the flight deck, listening to the pilot run up the engines and feeling her take off, as if she was floating on a breeze, brought back a flood of memories. It was my final mission and I got to share the moment with my sons and Mary Danielsen. On its approach to the Morristown Airport in the summer of 2012, the Collings Foundation's B-17 buzzed right over the top of my house. I could hear it sing from my living room. Meeting young soldiers on those tours made me realize how important it is to preserve one's personal military history as a part of our country's history. Every veteran should document his or her personal military biography with the Library of Congress Veterans History Project.

To fellow POW Ben H. Phelper for jogging my memory with his ground breaking book Kriege Memories. I believe we shared the same barracks.

To the Chatham (New Jersey) Historical Society, the Chatham Post Office and the Chatham Fire Department for being a big part of my life and my family.

To Lt. Raymond Bye, 2nd Lt. John J. Malik, 2nd Lt Meryl E. Woodside, 2nd Lt. William C. Kieran, Tech Sgt. Kenneth H. Nice, Staff Sgt. Frederick Holt, Staff Sgt. Charles C. Gattman, Staff Sgt. Michael Olynik, and Staff Sgt. Alton Baer Jr., for being my Air Force brothers. Still.

To my dear sweet wife Virginia for building a life with me that gave me a much bigger story to tell.

CONTENTS

Acknowledgements vii
1. Six of 11 1
2. Growing Up in Chatham 9
3. The Call to Serve 17
4. The Flying Fortress & The Mighty Eighth 27
5. The Crossing 43
6. The Theater 51
7. Black Thursday 63
8. Captured 77
9. Surviving Stalag XVII B 83
10. The Death March 99
11. Coming Home 109
12. My Virginia 119
13. Looking back 141
14. Reflections from my sons 143
Decorations & Citations 158
Military Medals 159
Honorary Discharge 160
Photography Captions & Credits 167
About the co-author 173

United States Air Force
Code of Ethics

Integrity First

Service Above Self

Excellence In All We Do.

FOREWORD

We heard our father's stories of serving in World War II in bits and pieces over the years. Every so often we would hear another story. Comparing them with the stories from a few dozen aunts, uncles and cousins, we understood the big picture.

This much we knew. One of the first in his 11-member family to be called to duty, Dad served as the top turret gunner in a four-engine B-17 heavy bomber in the United States Eight Air Force. He flew in the European theater, was shot down, and managed to survive being a prisoner of war for 24 months. The Germans nearly starved him to death. We knew about some of his missions, but not all of them. We even knew that, for a few years after the war, he visited occasionally with a fellow crew member.

We never really knew the whole story, however. We wanted to hear them all: From the little every day moments to the big mission battles. We wanted to know what it was like to be there, what it was like to take off from a grassy runway on a combat mission inside a B-17 flying fortress. As a family, we have toured restored B-17 bombers at air shows. While they were the most progressive machines of the day, by today's airplane standards they feel a little like a tin can inside. We will never know what it was really like to walk along the cat walk in the bomb bay while holding steady, or to sit curled up in position in the ball turret or stand for hours with hands double fisted on two machine guns peering out of the top turret. We will never know what it is like to fight for your life while bullets are raging in one side of the fuselage and out the other. We can only visualize what it must have been like for Dad and his crew to patrol the skies as German fighters came after them three and four at a time.

Only Dad's voice could put us there. This is a piece of our family history, our American history, and it needed to be preserved for future generations. We weren't sure, however, if Dad would sit down with us or anyone else and really open up about his war experiences. Fortunately, his memory is as sharp as a man 30 years his junior. We finally talked him into it.

Over a period of ten months Dad sat down with Mary Danielsen of Documented Legacy and they just talked. The more frequently they talked, the richer and more surprising the stories became. Dad's recollections inside the POW camp are as ingenious and amusing as they are horrific. What emerged and took shape was a story that went far beyond what we expected.

Dad had his own American dream that he wanted to fulfill. His faith helped him survive being a POW. He and our mother, Virginia Stanek Caporaso, saw that dream come true.

One of the biggest surprises about undertaking this project was that, through research, we were able to meet Brigid O'Donnell, daughter of Lt. Raymond Bye, the pilot of Crew K90. Lt. Bye served through two more wars and retired a colonel, a very honorable man. Dad always credited him with being the reason he's alive today. Lt. Bye's courageous calm and focus are most evident in Dad's stories of training and flying 10 combat missions. We are forever grateful to Brigid O'Donnell for her friendship and for sharing her father's military history, documents and photos to this project. Without her help, pieces of the story would have gone missing.

Every soldier has a story. Every veteran, who committed themselves to battle, has a deeply personal perspective of that moment in American history. This is Dad's story, told in his own words.

By Bob, Steve and Jim Caporaso

PROLOGUE

To my grandchildren's children,

When I was child, I never thought of growing up as anything that was difficult to do. I was born the sixth of 11 children and arrived in time to witness the Great Depression, when food and jobs were scarce. Our nation was struggling to overcome deep hardships. The suffering was evident in every town in America, even Chatham, New Jersey. In our home, we appreciated every little thing we had and we took nothing for granted.

My parents worked very hard to provide for us. It was a time of great ingenuity and thrift. My father worked as a gardener for the Lum family in Chatham and Mom was chief executive of our home. Together, they managed a well-organized backyard garden that kept us all fed and some of the neighbors, too. Yet, every one in my family contributed to the household. No exceptions. We went to school and did our work on time. If we were told to study, we studied. If we were told to write, we wrote. After school, we went straight home and did our homework, followed by our chores. If there was a way to earn extra money for the family, we did. Our elders were respected. On Sunday, we went to church. When the community rallied for a cause, we showed up. These were the tenets on which I grew up.

We did what we were expected to do.

This project was started with you in mind. I wanted you to see my life, hear my stories and know a little more about the path on which your story begins. I was honored to serve our country in the United States Army Air Force. I was lucky to come home alive.

When I was a child I never imagined that my entire life would be changed by war. It's not something I planned. Neither was it something that I was willing to talk about for many years. It is, however, what happens in life when you do what is expected: You grow up. I did.

My adult life had just started when I was drafted. My crew members and I were just kids then and the military trusted us to fly a million dollar airplane into the war. They put loads of responsibility on us. They trained us and trusted us. Yet, we were just kids, all except one under the age of 24. We may have been too young to grasp the weight of responsibility we carried. I don't know if that would happen again today.

I felt a sense of duty, as our country was at war. We wanted to get the war over and defeat our enemy. While serving, I had the opportunity to travel through different countries. The United States of America was and still is the greatest country in the world. I lost a lot of time in the prisoner of war camp, but I grew up in the process. Serving our country helped me understand the United States. It made me proud to be home. All I wanted to do was survive the war, come home to Chatham and begin the life I dreamed about living. We have a good country here. It's worth fighting for. If we ever had another war where I had to defend our country, I would be there again, if I could. I'd climb back into a B-17 in a second and wiggle my way up to the top turret. I'd find a way to serve.

Always remember this: The freedoms you enjoy as American citizens today were paid for by the sacrifices of others yesterday. Honor your home.

Love,
Gerard J. Caporaso
Master Sgt. USAF, Ret.

Chapter 1

SIX OF 11

P atrick, Thomas, Anna, Carmen, Anthony, Gerard, Lucy, Virginia, John, Mario and Elizabeth. The family lineup is easier to recite if you get into a rhythm.

Big families of five or more children were still the norm back when I was a kid. We didn't think anything of it, because most families around us were big. America was growing. So was Chatham, New Jersey.

My parents, Carmine and Carmela Caporaso, immigrated from Naples, Italy when they were both 17 years old. Dad, who became known as Frank Caporaso, arrived in 1906 and Mom in 1907. I don't know what brought them here or how they met. Their families were farmers. Mom and Dad married at the age of 20. Patrick followed. I was born Gerard Joseph Caporaso on June 15, 1921, right in the middle, the sixth of 11 altogether. It's hard for me to believe that seven of my siblings have already passed away. It feels like they are still here with me and we're all still talking about the family and growing up in Chatham.

By today's living standards, most people cannot imagine how a family of 11 children and two adults could survive in a small house. You have to remember the times we lived in. The Great Depression halted prosperity. Many people were out of work. Money was extremely tight or nonexistent. We didn't own a car. Even though my father worked, there wasn't any extra spending money. Nothing. My father and mother knew how to economize and make the most of a small amount of space. Every aspect of our lives became a big production, because of the volume of work it took to manage a household of 13 people.

Together we worked.

I grew up in a five-bedroom colonial home that sat on a 25 by 100-foot lot at the upper end of a dead-end street. South Passaic Avenue was a dirt road when I was born. It didn't have sidewalks going all the way up the street. We had a sidewalk in front of our property and the neighbors next door did, too. The dead end gave us the freedom to play outside in the street where we spent hours playing kick the can, kick ball, hide-and-seek, and the human chain-link game Red Rover. It was a good street for young families.

Our house sat at the front end of the property, elevated from its neighbors, and had a small screened-in front porch. My father planted an apple tree in the front lawn just a few feet off the road, and took care to spray and prune it yearly. The apples were always crisp and delicious.

To the left of our front yard was a flat grassy area where my father and our Italian relatives played bocce ball. Today it's a driveway, void of all memories of our competitiveness and laughter. Concerned with rainwater runoff pouring into his yard, our neighbor installed a concrete detaining wall on the property line between our houses. Dad wasn't thrilled about it, because the neighbor cut down a row of trees, but, I must say, the three-foot high wall did stop the bocce balls from rolling into his yard.

People always want to know where we put everyone.

On the third floor of our home - the attic level - we had two completed bedrooms. Three brothers slept in the back bedroom in a double and a single bed. My oldest brother, Patrick, took the smaller front bedroom with a single bed. When he married and moved out, I eventually took that bedroom.

There were three bedrooms and a full bathroom on the second floor. My parents had the front bedroom. My two sisters had one bedroom with two double beds and the remaining three brothers took the last bedroom, which also had a double and a single bed. The rooms always seemed to be filled. By the time the younger children were born, several of my older siblings had already married. For instance, my oldest sister Anna married before my youngest sister Betty was born. As such, we never had four girls in one bedroom.

We shared everything, however.

The main floor of the house had a living room, bedroom and the kitchen, which ran the width of the house and about one-third deep. When I was growing up we didn't have electricity in the house. We had gas jets that lighted the rooms. As we needed them, we would turn the gas jets on and light them. When electricity came out my father had the electric light put in, but he kept the gas jets in the kitchen and one bedroom.

Most people can't imagine living without electricity, especially today when our lives are so dependent on gadgets that require us to be plugged in. The only heat in the house came from the kitchen and rose up through a heat vent in the ceiling to warm the upper bedrooms. As a family, we made it work and learned to dress warmly.

My mother managed the household and everything happened through the kitchen. She was a fantastic cook. Her entire day revolved around cooking and baking for all of us. I won't say I was Mom's favorite child, but I was one of her favorites. She took care of me all the time.

We had a big black cast iron stove in the kitchen. Every Saturday I used to have to paint it jet black and polish it up really nice. We had trouble getting wood started in that coal stove. We couldn't burn coal in it 24 hours a day. It was too expensive. To economize, we burned wood in it to heat the house and coal when we needed to cook.

Painting the stove black seems like such a silly chore, but it was one of the many chores that had to be done in our house every week. There were other assignments, like taking out the ashes, chopping wood and all that kind of stuff that went with it.

Every one who lived there worked there.

We had a ceramic-topped table in our kitchen that could seat eight to 10 people around it: three on each side and two on each end. We could squeeze a few more people in if we had to. With all that cooking there were loads of pots and pans to clean up after we ate together. Mom didn't do any of the cleanup work. We did.

We all had different chores. One of them was to clean off the table. One of them was to wash the dishes. Another was to clean and dry the dishes. Another was to sweep the floors, while others washed or dried the pots and pans. Everybody got assigned one of those details. They weren't big, but they were necessary for every meal. No matter who was eating someone got those details. If there weren't enough people, you got more than one chore.

My father worked as a gardener and chauffeur for Chatham attorney Charles M. Lum and his family. He wasn't paid much money, but Mr. Lum employed him throughout the Great Depression. As such, my mother was able to cook meals that would satisfy all of us. She cooked stews and macaroni, meals that would last for a few days. We would eat one dish one day and then maybe not the next day, but on the day after we would have some more. It was hard for her. She didn't have much money to buy food.

Grocery shopping was another production in planning. Food my mother always needed in the house was purchased in big bulk sizes, mostly from Esposito's grocery in Madison. An Italian grocer would come in and take an order on Tuesday and deliver it on Thursday. He'd get another order and return it the following Tuesday. That went on for years that I know. Since she cooked everything from scratch, including baking her own bread, she regularly bought 100-pound bags of flour and sugar and a gallon of olive oil at a time.

In the fall, she would buy 1,000 pounds of potatoes and other canned goods for the winter. We had a shelf in the basement where we stored all the potatoes. They came in a big sack and we'd open them up and spread them out. Whenever we wanted to cook some, we just went downstairs and got a few. The shelf was next to a large bench where we stored all the canned goods.

In the spring my mother always made her own lard. She bought fat back and boiled it and boiled it. She poured the melted fat into these huge vats in the kitchen and, once they hardened, we had lard all year long. These are the things that you don't see anymore.

In the summer time my mother canned a lot of peaches, pears, tomatoes, and peppers in jars. We helped her peel the fruits and stuff. Cut it up. In those days a farmer used to come around with a truck load of peaches. He would ride down the street yelling, "Peaches, peaches." People in the neighborhood knew his routine. They would go out and buy whatever baskets they wanted, right on the street. We always bought whatever Mom wanted to can, so we'd have fruit all winter long. She used to always do that kind of stuff. Another farmer would come around in a truck and sell us vegetables every week. He liked our big family and my mother was his customer for a long time.

The family recipe we still talk about is my mother's Italian Easter pie, which is also known as Italian meat pie. There are two distinct ways to cook an Easter pie: layered in a tower of pie crust cooked in a spring-form baking pan or mixed together and cooked in a pie pan. Mom cooked them as pies. The center was filled with a ricotta, parmesan, and mozzarella mixture layered with strips of prosciutto, chunks of Genoa salami and ham. Depending on how you made it, the pie was cooked with either three or 10 eggs beaten into the mixture. Sometimes eggs were hard boiled and put into the middle. Sometimes spinach was mixed into it. You could smell the crust baking from down the street and we all lined up for them.

Mom used to make a whole bunch of them in big pie pans every Easter. She made smaller ones for my sisters - the ones who were married. They were expensive, too. Oh, I still love them. I'd always be there at the kitchen table when she started making them. But I just did my part of the production and never really paid attention to exactly how to cook an Easter pie. I should have, so I would know exactly how Mom cooked hers. She made it the same way every time, but I didn't know how to cook it or how many eggs to put in it. I knew what went in it, because I would cut up the salami for her. She used to get sticks of salami and cheeses and I would cut them into chunks for her. We'd add the prosciutto, which was expensive, and the ham. They were good. Every Easter I would come out to help her, but we couldn't sample the pies until Easter dinner.

My mother's recipes were gold. When she passed away, my sister Lucy grabbed the Easter pie recipe and wouldn't share it with the rest of the family. I finally said to her, "What's the story? It's not your recipe. It's your mother's." I suppose she just didn't want anyone to have it.

My mother made pizza long before there ever were pizza stores around. She cooked the sauce all day and made the dough from scratch. One day a friend of mine, who lived two doors away, came over. I asked him if he wanted a piece of pizza.

He said, "A piece of what? What's that?"

"A piece of pizza. It's good."

"All right I will try it," he said.

I always said that my mother made the first pizza in Chatham, long before any of these other places opened up. My friend admitted that she was one of the first. With a mother who is a good cook, neighborhood friends know to hang around – there's always a good meal not far away.

Our family kitchen was unforgettable. The room was about 15 feet by 20 feet in size, the largest room in the house. We usually had a Catholic calendar on the wall, one we got at church. The table was right in the center. After dinner and chores, we did our homework around that table.

There was a little room off the side of the kitchen with a John in it and we had a cubbyhole on the side that held an old fashion ice box. We used to buy ice every day from Green's Ice House. The ice man would make his way down the street and we would buy a 15-cent piece or a 10-cent piece. Whatever was needed. On weekends or holidays we bought a bigger piece that lasted a few days. We could buy a whole block of ice, but often we just needed a small piece. He would just break one off.

Of course, the milk man came around a couple of times a week, too. The milk came in glass quarts with paper caps. If you didn't get out to get the milk bottles early enough in the winter, the cream would either come out of the top or break the glass. It wouldn't go to waste. My mother would just cut it off and we'd have cream. It was delicious!

All of our dishes and utensils were stored in a giant closet in the kitchen. Pots and pans went down underneath. In the kitchen we had a sink. Next to it was a two-bin washing tub where my mother did the wash. She had a scrub board and, occasionally we used to help her wash the clothes. My mother hung everything out to dry on two clothes lines out back: one upstairs off the back porch, which extended from my brothers' bedroom, and one downstairs. She hung the sheets out in the fresh air all the time.

My Dad's ability to turn soil and seeds into an abundance of fruits, vegetables and flowers that provided for two households was a gift. He knew how to work the dirt. His strength was his ability to manage a large amount of elegantly maintained property for Mr. Lum and then come home to garden the small space of our family's back yard. He was skilled enough to put every inch of soil to work for us. That kept us fed when so many others went hungry.

When we were young kids - maybe in grammar school - my father used to grow tomatoes in the back yard. He had a couple of hundred plants. During the growing season he would take the best seedlings for our yard and then give the remaining plants to neighbors and area businessmen. They looked forward to his good castoffs.

The family garden took over our whole backyard. We had the two back porches. In the summertime we slept out on the upstairs back porch to stay cool. We had a grape arbor that extended off the upper porch about 10 feet. At the end of it was a fence that sectioned off the remaining yard for the garden. We had grapes galore: purple grapes and white grapes. When the grapes fell, the bees came buzzing.

My father grew other things besides tomatoes, such as lettuce, celery, zucchini, green beans, and carrots, but mostly tomatoes. He knew just how to stake the tomatoes to get the biggest yield from each plant. Everything was planted in perfectly neat rows. He always had a fig plant, too. They were warm weather plants, so in the winter he would wrap the fig trees with tar paper and fill the inside with leaves to keep them warm. Sure enough, every year they came back. We loved figs in the summer time.

We had our share of wine, too. My mother and father had Italian friends in the area who made their own wine. My father would get a gallon every so often.

At some point every summer we had more vegetables than we could eat or can. Mom would wash up a bunch of tomatoes and put them on a plate. She'd clean them up good. We'd walk around the neighborhood, house to house, selling them for 10 cents, 15 cents or a quarter, depending on the size of the tomatoes. They were good tomatoes. Because my father knew how to grow them well, people would buy them.

Mom saved all that tomato money and used it to buy her potatoes and canned goods in the fall. Even though she canned her own tomatoes, she still bought tomato sauce in bulk for the winter months. She used to buy gallons of black olives and 50 or 100-pound bags of white beans. She bought spaghetti that came loose and not in a package. She always had food in the house that allowed her to make a quick meal.

Chicken, spaghetti and meatballs. Oh, I miss those days.

While it was home, the house in Chatham had too many stairs for my mother. As she grew older her varicose veins made it difficult for her to manage the stairs. About the time my wife Virginia and I began searching for a home my father saw that new ranch-style homes were being built in Summit in the early 1950s. So, he sold the family home and moved.

My childhood revolved around a home buzzing with activity. Each of us had our own responsibilities, but we always came together for meals, school, church, family time and the community. Our love and dedication to each other was unwavering.

Living in tight quarters in a large family made training in the Air Force easier. I was already accustomed to being in a crowd. Food was such a big part of the culture of my family, not by volume or by choice of food but rather by how we came together for food, that when it was denied to me for such a long period of time during the war it was a wound that never quite healed. The culture of my family helped keep me alive during my time in World War II. My experiences abroad, however, defined the way I chose to live the rest of life.

Chapter 2

GROWING UP IN CHATHAM

Chatham is home for me. Rolled into the work ethic on which we were raised are all these deeply cherished family memories of how we lived from the 1920s to the 1940s.

When my father immigrated to this country he began working as a gardener on an estate in Madison, New Jersey, the city known for its roses. Eventually he was offered a job working as a gardener and chauffeur for Charles M. Lum in Chatham, and moved downtown. They were old money folks: the Lums and the Budds.

My father's hands could make things grow. He knew how to work the land naturally, the old fashion way. He understood companion planting, and how to stimulate garden beds to create a vibrant array of flowers, shrubs and produce year round. Sometimes he also did stonework on the properties. Whatever needed to be done.

Every morning when he left the house, if he didn't cut through our neighbor's yard on the path alongside their two-stall garage, he walked down to Second Street and up to Fairmount Avenue.

The Lum family lived about a half mile away at 87 Fairmount Avenue, just across from Oliver Street, in a traditional Foursquare Colonial with a sprawling front porch and wide steps that greeted guests in a yard framed with pristinely pruned bushes and flower beds. The original property was larger back then, maybe an acre or two in size. The front yard sloped down to the sidewalk where my father lined the walkway with annual flower beds. There were all kinds of flowers, annuals that were fashionable in the day.

Their lawn was big, both front and back. At that point in the growing season when there was more work than hours in the day able to accomplish everything, I used to help my father cut the grass and rake the leaves when I was little. I helped him in the garden, too, when he was pulling weeds. Behind the Lum's house were woods that rolled all the way down hill to Fuller Avenue. South on Fuller, just before the keyhole of a dead end, were a row of greenhouses on the right side of the street.

My father was kept very busy. The extended Lum family owned a large farm that encompassed six city blocks, about 1.8 miles around. It ran from Inwood Road south to Longwood Avenue between Washington and Lafayette avenues. Today that farm hosts Chatham High School, Lafayette Elementary School and several hundred homes in the square that includes Dellwood Avenue, Fairview Avenue, Chandler Road and Oak Road.

There were several Lum families in town and each of them owned a piece of the farm. Each household had a gardener, who managed their private section. As far as I remember, there were no homes on any of that property, except for a small barn that housed a horse owned by one of the Lum girls. Her family lived on Chandler Road. As a matter of fact, I was named Gerard after her brother.

In addition to all the work he had to accomplish at the main house, my father cultivated the Lum's farm property, growing all their fruits and vegetables. He planted for them, but he planted for us there, too. We always had fresh produce from the Lum's garden.

My family had some nice routines.

Growing up, I attended St. Patrick's School through the eighth grade, graduating in a class of nine - five girls and four boys - in 1935. In the morning I'd cut through my neighbor's yard, using the path on the side of the garage, crossing the vacant lot behind it and Fairmount Avenue before walking a long block up Chatham Street to school. I'd cut through the grass playing field on the side of the school where the parking lot now sits and make it to class before the morning lesson. There were fewer cars on the road back then, since they were still considered a huge luxury. I could make it to school fast.

On the way home I'd pass a couple of houses at either end of Chatham Street that had apple trees in the front yard. I'd often help myself. They were the greatest, most crisp apples.

Founded in 1872 by a group of families that wanted a stronger Catholic education for their children, the school was originally housed inside the gothic brick church building at the corner of Oliver Street and Washington Avenue. It was a nice church, but it was small. The first 160 parishioners to arrive on Sunday got a seat. The rest had to stand against the walls. I was an altar boy there. My wife and I got married in that church. It's now a nursery school.

The nuns from the Sisters of Charity, who taught at the school, lived in a donated convent next door. The first school building, a wooden structure dating back to 1887, was built on the site of the present church and rectory. That building was torn down in 1931, while I was attending school there, and a new building was erected.

We had no sports teams at the school. The only physical education-type classes that were taught were held in a large meeting room in the basement. We could play most sports down there, except basketball. The rough old dirty field that now holds the parking lot is where we played baseball and made a mess.

Looking back, I attended school while the community was experiencing real growing pains. Its ranks swelled to about 3,000 residents, which was big at the time. We had about a third of the homes that exist today. As a child, this expansion was most evident in the classroom.

One teacher taught two grades together: fifth and sixth grades, for instance. It wasn't hard for them to juggle the grades. While the teacher taught one grade a lesson, the other grade was either taking a test, reading or working on another lesson. You never opened your mouth in class or you got smacked with the ruler. She switched off between the grades throughout the day. We did all our work in school.

St. Patrick School still only teaches to the eighth grade. There wasn't a Catholic high school in town. After I graduated elementary school I went to the Chatham High School, a block from home. I remember the nuns taunting us about doing a good job on our work and studying hard. They terrified us.

"When you get to high school you'll be the dumbest kids there," I remember them saying when I was in the seventh grade.

My freshmen year in high school I was one of the smartest students in my class. I didn't have to worry about anything. I was an honor roll student and graduated high school in 1939. Maybe it was all that ruler beating or the fact that we worked hard.

The original high school is now the Chatham Municipal Building. While I was there the town went through another growth spurt. A larger high school building was built behind it on school property between Fairmount and Lum avenues. For a while we were on split sessions: morning and afternoon. They would change every three or four months, so that students could switch.

We never had nothing to do.

You see, we didn't have television in those days. Since we didn't have electricity in the house, we hooked a radio up to a car battery. My oldest brother, Patrick, liked to tinker with cars. It was his hobby. He had to charge the battery when it went weak while it was hooked up to the radio.

We listened to programs such as The Lone Ranger, the Hit Parade, and Amos 'n' Andy, which my father liked. Every night at 6:45, Dad sat down to listen to the evening news. He leaned into the radio, hanging on every word from Walter Winchell, the news and gossip commentator.

As I grew up, the four oldest kids got married. Even though they moved out and started their own homes, they always came back for Sunday dinner. Afterward, we cleared off the dinner dishes and turned the house into a pinochle tournament. My father loved pinochle and my sister and brothers did, too. We always had three or four pinochle games going on. That was a big thing in those days for us: coming back for meals and playing pinochle. We played cards for a dime. So, if you lost a quarter in a card game on Sunday afternoon it wasn't a big deal.

We appreciated everything we had, especially each other. We were a closely knit family. You can't buy that with money, no matter what generation you are living in.

At Christmas time we were lucky if we got one toy. We were lucky if the boys got one truck and my sisters got one doll. It's not like today where kids get hundreds of dollars worth of Christmas toys.

At one time, there was a minor league baseball team in Chatham. When you were old enough you could chase balls for them for a quarter. We used to chase balls into the woods. Occasionally, we couldn't find one. Eventually, we'd go back to find it so we had a ball to play with. We didn't have any bats, however. Sometimes we would get a broken or cracked bat from a player. We just put a screw and a few nails in it. We would use that bat. We weren't hitting it that hard anyhow.

As the years went on, we got a pair of roller skates that would clamp onto your feet. We would wear out the wheels. We used to have to go to the bike shop for new ones. Ten cents a wheel. Those were the days. Things were a little cheaper.

We didn't have the problems that kids have today. We made our own sports. We had a scroungy looking football that we played with. Sometimes we shot marbles. Sometimes the girls played jump rope. In the springtime, we flew kites. Of course, we made our own. I was good at kite flying. I always had one way up in the air.

That reminds me of the time my son Bob was in the YMCA Indian Guides and the pack had a kite flying contest at the Short Hills Mall before the mall was built up like it is now. We had the highest kite in the air. There were a bunch of guys flying kites, who didn't know what they were doing. They got their kites tangled with ours and they cut our string. Can you imagine that? They cut our string. Our kite went flying over the golf course at Canoe Brook Country Club. I was mad as heck and cursed that guy out.

I said, "Come on Bob. Let's go get it."

So we went down to the golf course and rode along the road, down by the 18th hole, just as that kite started coming down. A golfer was riding along the golf course, holding the string, which was heavy, and playing golf. It was the funniest sight. Bob still had it the next time he went to an Indian Guides meeting. He got a trophy for the highest flying kite. He's proud of that one.

Those are things we did.

By the time I was paying attention to my grown-up brothers, they were already working jobs in the neighborhood. Patrick became an adult when I was seven years old. Thomas was two years younger than him. Carmen was five years older than me and Anthony was just two years older. My brothers used to give part of their paychecks to Mom, to help with food and expenses. They didn't earn much money, maybe $20 a week. They would give her $10 or $15. I used to tell them, "You've got to give her more than that."

Another brother worked as a caddy at a golf course. When he came home he would give her a couple of bucks from what he earned.

I used to deliver newspapers from 6 a.m. until it was time to go to high school and then again in the afternoon with a paper dealer in Chatham. I got paid $5 a week. As a side job I also folded the advertising inserts for the Sunday papers on Wednesdays. That earned me an extra quarter each week. I'd give Mom the $5 and kept the 25 cents.

That was the late 1930's. Things were tough.

Gerard Caporaso, back row third from the right,
with his Boy Scout troop in the 1930s.

Downtown Chatham, New Jersey, circa 1930's.

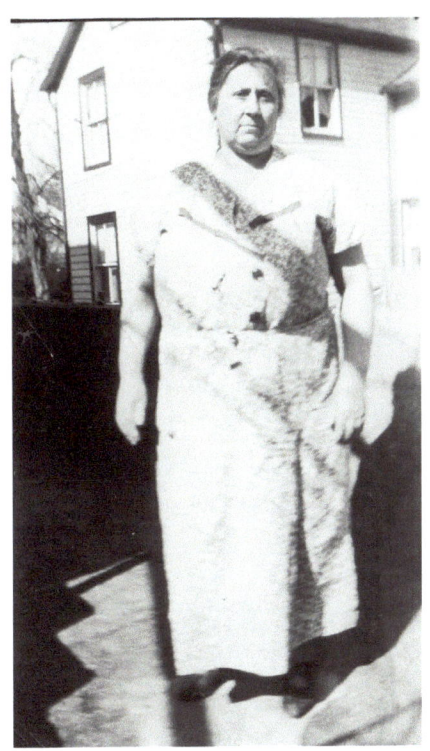

Carmela Caporaso (right) and Carmine "Frank" Caporaso (below), Gerard Caporaso's parents in the late 1930's.

Chapter 3

THE CALL TO SERVE

I never talked about my military service until recent years. Most men of my generation didn't talk about it. We found it better to move on. That is, of course, unless we met up with other veterans and began commiserating about our experiences, as men of a certain age do. Still, there were the stories you told and the stories you never repeated.

The war had just started when I was drafted. I had graduated high school just a few years earlier and had a part time job. I was 21 years old, old enough to be a man and too young to be frightened by the journey that lay ahead.

While I was waiting to be called up for duty, I got a job working for the Car General Insurance Company in downtown Manhattan. Every morning I walked a few blocks from my home to the little station off Main Street in Chatham, and loaded the train that carried businessmen to their offices in Newark and New York. I worked long hours and came home at 8 or 9 o'clock at night. As much as I loved the steady work, the lengthy hours and travel weren't working for me. So, I quit that job.

It was hard for me to get another job, because I was in the service. I wasn't officially called to duty yet, but I was drafted and I had lower draft numbers. Every potential boss knew that when the notice finally came in, I would be gone. It's hard to maintain a stable workforce that way. The manager at the Woolworth store in Millburn finally hired me. I worked there until I went into the service.

I was in the Morris County group of recruits. When the notice finally came that I must report for duty I was sent to Madison for a physical. Afterward, our group was sent home for a few days off. The send off was a bit hectic. We reported back to Madison and then were taken to Newark. My family came to see me off there for the last time.

We were sent to Fort Dix in Pemberton, New Jersey for our initial training. After filling out a pile of paperwork, I was issued my serial number: 32461208. Name, rank and serial number are all you are ever allowed to reveal to the enemy. A solider never forgets his number.

At a briefing at Fort Dix we were asked what we wanted to be. For some reason I said the Air Force. At that time, they needed air crews and gunners. They said the life of a gunner was only seconds, not even minutes. Being a crewmen in the U.S. Army Air Corps wasn't something you were assigned. You had to ask for it and you had to qualify to serve.

A month into service all the new Army Air Force recruits were sent to Florida for testing. It was still a new facility. There were a lot of questions we had to answer.

In our first meeting there, an officer got up and announced they needed gunners and they wanted people to sign up for the positions. A half dozen people in my group signed up. To be a radio operator you had to pass that test. There was a teacher in my group, who could play the piano. He was great at reading radio code. The mechanical test was good for me, because I understood the gears and stuff. I easily passed the mechanics test. After all the testing they sent me to air mechanics training school in Amarillo, Texas.

Having never ventured far from my hometown of Chatham, I was suddenly zigzagging the country with a duffle bag full of government-issued possessions. It was both tremendously exciting and scary. Everything was new and unfamiliar. Even if I was just peering out a troop train window, I got to see how families live in other regions of this vast country.

The AM (air mechanics) school had just opened before my group arrived. It was in a constant state of construction. It was muddy. They had no boardwalk boards down, yet. When you walked around you had to roll your pants up, otherwise you'd get loaded with mud. I was there training in different classes for over half a year. It went fast. I learned about ammunition and bombs and stuff. There they had three classes a day, eight hours a day. We worked around the clock, changing shifts: 8 a.m. - 4 p.m., 4 p.m. - 12 a.m. and 12 a.m - 8 a.m. Every month or so we were transferred to another shift. This way everyone wouldn't get the early shift.

> Opened in April 1942 under the command of Col. Edward C. Black, the Amarillo Army Air Field was a 1,523-acre facility located approximately six miles east of the City of Amarillo on the boundary of Potter and Randall counties in the High Plains of the Texas Panhandle.
>
> Construction on the buildings was only half completed when the first classes began to arrive in September 1942. The field, one of the largest installations in the Western Technical Training Command, was established for training of air crew and ground mechanics to service the B-17 Flying Fortress aircraft.
>
> Between 1943 and 1945, the facility expanded rapidly to include basic training and special instruction courses. It was later designated to train technicians and flight engineers for the B-29 aircraft. Flying operations were inaugurated, and basic military training began at the base in the spring of 1943.

It was a good school. I may still have boxes in the basement of my home with training manuals that I sent home. We always had to draw pictures of something or another - parts of the plane. We were constantly and consistently tested on all areas of the plane's mechanics. We had to know it blind. The instructors checked our work and retested us until everyone got it right.

One day after our morning classes a group of us buddies decided to go horseback riding in Palo Duro Canyon State Park, which was a fairly new 20,000-acre destination just south of Amarillo. We all thought we were John Wayne, riding high in the saddle in full uniform under the hot desert sun. The horses we rented there were so familiar with the trails that they led us. They paraded us down around the red-dirt mountains into the dusty canyon where we came upon a wild pig. I was the only one in our group with a camera. We took photos all afternoon in our very best western poses.

We were in Amarillo for Thanksgiving. Our dinner was at midnight, because we worked in three different shifts. A friend from New Providence, who went in the service with me, had some family friends living down there. One of them, Mrs. F. Poltler, invited him to her home for another Thanksgiving dinner the next day.

He brought me along. We got to eat our second holiday dinner with her husband and baby daughter Gail.

I remember the night before - Thanksgiving Eve - it snowed like heck. It was deep. By lunchtime the next day it all melted. It was a crazy thing.

After we finished school in Amarillo we were sent to Seattle, Washington to the Boeing plant for more training in January 1943. That's when we knew we would be flying B-17s. The remainder of our group was sent to train on B-24s.

Interestingly enough, when we traveled from Florida to Amarillo, Texas we went in a troop train and ate in the box car. When we were sent to Seattle, we traveled on a regular passenger train and ate in the dining car.

When we arrived the entire City of Seattle was closed up. A snow storm had blown through, dumping three or four inches of snow over the city. We didn't know it until we got there, but Seattle is all hills. A little bit of snow would shut down the whole town.

We were there for a month or six weeks. We were like kids testing out new toys. We saw real B-17s, new ones just coming off the line. We got our first training on the Flying Fortress there. It was really good.

It was time to put all this training into practice.

From Seattle we were sent to Las Vegas for gunnery practice. They flew us up in AT-6s. It was an open cockpit plane with two cockpits: one in the front and one in the back. We were in the back. We shot at a tow target pulled by another plane. They kept our scores by giving us different colored bullets. Each time we went up we were given a different color. We didn't know that at first. It became obvious: the red bullets left distinct red marks on the target and the blue ones left blue marks.

> Known as "the pilot maker," the North American Aviation AT-6 was a spitfire of a warbird. It was the single engine trainer aircraft used to train pilots of the United States Air Force and Navy, and the Royal Air Force. It is commonly known by a variety of designations depending on the model and operating air force. At 29 feet long with a 42-foot wing span, the AT-6 could travel over 200 miles per hour.

The first time I went up for target practice the AT-6 was an open cockpit. I was strapped in. To shoot, I had to unhook my safety harness on one side, stand up, shoot at the target, wiggle my gun and then sit back down and strap myself in. The first time we did that it was all right. When I wiggled the gun and motioned to sit back down I felt a sudden deafening drop. Zoom! The pilot decided to play a little joke on me and nosedive a machine the size of a flatbed truck. I heaved all the way down. After landing I was sent to the base doctor, who was going to wash me out.

"I don't want to be washed out."

"Are you sure," he asked?

"Yes, I'm sure."

He gave me some seasickness pills and told me to take one every time I went up. I never took the pills and never got sick again throughout the whole war. It was great.

The second time we went up to shoot I didn't wiggle the gun. I sat down first, hooked up my safety harness and only then did I wiggle the gun. The pilot could do whatever he wanted to do. After that I was pretty good.

Throughout our training, we were tested in different planes and in different positions. The ball turret position was the one that was too cramped for me. I couldn't get in there and, if I did, I couldn't move too much. I was glad I didn't get that position.

Apparently I did well in my mechanics training. When I came out of gunnery school we were all promoted to sergeants. We were sent to the airfield in Dalhart, Texas in the Northwest corner of the Texas Panhandle where my crew was formed from the group that trained together. I was made a technical sergeant. Since I got an extra rank I figured I got the top turret position, too. That's where the flight engineer went. The rest of the crew - minus the pilot and co-pilot - were staff sergeants.

We did a little training in Dalhart, but not much.

While we were only there a short time, our newly formed crew took some official flights together. The training was focused on getting members used to their positions. Initially we had eleven members assigned to the crew, but my buddy Paul Paradee was assigned to pilot training school. He was only with us a short time. Lt. John J. Malik took his post as co-pilot. Once that change was made everyone stayed together. We never were substituted out to fill in for another crew that was short handed.

Our pilot was Lt. Raymond F. Bye. Lt. John Malik was the co-pilot. The navigator was 2nd Lt. Meryl Woodside and the bombardier was 2nd Lt. William C. Kieran. Our crew of staff sergeants included Frederick Holt as the ball turret gunner, Charles C. Gattman and Michael Olynik as waist gunners and Alton Baer

Jr. as the tail gunner. Kenneth Nice and I were both technical sergeants. I was the top turret gunner and he served as the radio operator.

We were young kids in our early 20's, except the navigator, who was 27. We thought he was an old man. We were in our glory doing what we wanted to do. We didn't worry about anything. We had no fear of flying or going into the compound or attacking enemy targets. For me it was great. I enjoyed flying very much. I'd like to be that young again and to be flying again.

We had a good crew. Everyone got along real well.

Lt. Malik was young too, maybe 22. He was a good friend. The fact that Malik was a lieutenant didn't make a difference in our friendship. He and Sgt. Baer would go out a lot, but not often. Meryl Woodside was a little standoffish, like the pilot. We didn't have a lot to do with him. Bill Kieran and I were close. He was all right. After the war he lived in Livingston, New Jersey and we got together every once in a while for dinner. Occasionally, I would do stuff with Bill, Charles Gattman, and Fred Holt.

Alton Baer knew how to liven up the action: as much as you can when you are training in the middle of the desert and living between combat missions. He was the good looking ladies' man from the Midwest, who always had a few girlfriends. I knew him quite well. Throughout our training Alton always managed to find a way to sneak out or go to town and meet up with the ladies. When we flew to St. Louis and eventually Bangor, Maine we were not supposed to leave the base.

He would say, "Come on. I'll show you."

Next thing I knew we were all filing behind him like ducklings as he took us to a fence and showed us how to get out under it. We'd sneak into town and find a rink where we would skate around for a while before going out again. At 21, he sure knew how to get around. And he knew the girls! He managed to find all the dances at the Red Cross halls, both here and abroad, where we met girls. It was good.

Lt. Bye was more or less aloof. We didn't have a lot to do with him socially, but the other three officers we did. There had to be a dividing line between his authority and his friendships.

The camaraderie of a flight crew is a study in human nature. We lived together for a year in training. It was a long courtship. We worked in close quarters and our lives depended on each other. Yet there were rules we had to follow. Commissioned officers and noncommissioned officers (noncoms) were not supposed to socialize together. Lt. Malik would sneak out occasionally with Alton Baer and me. Yet, we had a very good crew. We were very friendly with each other. We used to play cards together. Sometimes we shot dice.

THE CALL TO SERVE

When we went to England they paid us in English currency. We were hunkered under the plane waiting for something to happen. I can't remember what. We had nothing to do and we always had dice with us. So, we started a dice game. It ended up we were putting in English pound notes, which were worth four American dollars. It looked like a dollar to us. The five pound note was worth $20. We were throwing that in, too. We didn't know what we were betting, even though we thought we were betting dollars and five dollars. It turns out I won about $600 that night. That was the only time I won big like that.

We received one pass - one mini vacation - while we were stationed in Amarillo, Texas. It wasn't long, but I decided to fly home and fly back. I'd rather spend it with my family in Chatham.

There were more rattlesnakes than people in Pyote, Texas. It was a hot dry place when we arrived there from Dalhart in the late spring of 1943. Pyote is a 354-mile straight shot south of Dalhart, anchored to the southeastern corner of New Mexico.

It was a very small town surrounded by wide open territory. Our base was a just a great big field with runways. Except for the sight of electrical wires weaving across the street, everywhere you looked was vast open land. It was open though for planes to fly. We had lots of room to stretch our wings. There was a tiny little strip of a downtown, but we never saw it. There just wasn't much around.

In Pyote, we were conducting training flights where we were flying over the mountains in western Texas and circling back through Oklahoma before dropping a certain number of bombs over a designated target.

One day we took off from the airfield using a small prop propeller plane. Aircraft that used propellers as their primary propulsion device relied on piston engines to get virtually all of their thrust from the propeller driven by the engine. While these planes weren't known for their great speed, historically they played a significant part in World War II as both escort spitfires and general aviation planes. This one was an older model prop plane. The runways weren't paved yet, just pure southwestern dirt. On that particular day we may have even been taking off on a runway covered in truck tracks. As we moved down the runway in Pyote, we needed all pistons firing. It wasn't happening. We just about cleared the telephone wires and other equipment at the end of the field when we realized we couldn't control the plane. It was a runaway.

"We're going back to get it fixed," Lt. Bye said as he rushed to turn the prop around.

"Oh, I can fix that. It's easy." I remember the mechanic saying. About an hour later he called and gave us the all-clear sign to fly again. The propeller could be adjusted for pitch, but the mechanic on the ground didn't do it. He never fixed the problem. The pilot got us up in the air, realized the problem still existed, and coming back we barely cleared the landing zone. We nearly hit all the electrical wires again. Lt. Bye was mad as heck.

"This is it! We're not flying any more today."

So we took the day off.

The thought of nearly crashing on a training mission was and wasn't scary. Because we were up in the air and we cleared the wires, the rest of the crew was focused on our tasks. At the time, we didn't realize that we could have hit those wires and crashed. After we landed the second time we realized just how lucky we were to clear them. We finally understood the pilot and co-pilot's fear.

The night of July 17, 1943 we flew up in a thunder storm that wouldn't let up. It pounded us like an enemy. I thought we were going to get killed there. A good friend of mine, Staff Sgt. Victor Carozzo of Montchanin, Delaware, someone I spent a lot of time with during training, was also flying that night. His plane crashed in the mountains of western Texas, near Logan, New Mexico and the entire crew was killed. It was a week before he was supposed to go on furlough to be married. It was heartbreaking. I lost a bunch of good friends that night. We were lucky. Lt. Bye was a good pilot. He got us back safely that night.

Oh, I always wanted to fly as a young kid. I used to build little model airplanes, the ones you built with little rubber bands.

For training we flew different types of airplanes and we'd fly in different positions. I flew in the bomb bay and I flew in the turret. I didn't particularly care for the ball turret, because it's kind of crowded. It's snug, you know. It's just as good as a top turret, because you could see down below.

We flew different types of planes: one-engine planes and two-engine planes. That was to just get us accustomed to flying. Once our crew was formed and we were assigned to B-17s in Seattle then we only flew B-17s. That was our thing.

Prior to that, when we went to ground gunnery school, we had all types of gunnery instruction. We had machine guns on the ground we had to shoot at a moving target. A truck even stood on the back of another truck and had a shot gun attached to shoot at clay pigeons. The targets were set up on a course. We rode around on the back of a truck and shot at it.

After a year in the states where our training was fine tuned and choreographed to the point where we could recite our routines in our sleep, it was time to go to work.

When the order came we flew an older model B-17 to Lambert Field in St. Louis, Missouri, which is now known as Lambert-St. Louis International Airport. The airport is about ten miles north west of the downtown. During the war the area became an aviation manufacturing hub for McDonnell Aircraft (now Boeing), Robertson Aircraft Corporation and Curtiss-Wright Corporation. Together they manufactured more than 3,000 airplanes for the war. We were sent there to pick up a brand new Boeing B-17 and fly it over to the Glasgow Prestwick Airport in Prestwick, Scotland, where the U.S. Air Force had a base during the war. Even though it was a new plane, its electronics were already outdated. It was scheduled to be retrofit.

We thought that was going to be our plane. Lt. Bye had planned to name it the Outhouse Mouse in reference to an expression our original co-pilot used. In his pocket on the flight over Lt. Bye carried a drawing of the nose art he wanted painted on the plane. It was a picture of a mouse peeking around the corner of an outhouse. Unfortunately for us, we didn't get to keep the plane. We'll never know if our Outhouse Mouse is the famous Outhouse Mouse, which was one of the longest serving airships in the war and credited with being the first heavy bomber to receive an attack by a German jet during the August 16th mission to the Siebel aircraft factory in Halle.

Our pilot was from New York. We were scheduled to fly to Bangor, Maine and then over to Scotland. As we took off from Chicago, Lt. Bye announced that we were flying through Bangor, but first he wanted to buzz his hometown on Staten Island in New York. He wanted to circle around town, flying low, and make enough noise for people to notice. Hopefully, someone might know it was him.

I asked, "Can you buzz my hometown, too?" He said all right.

I told him where I lived and helped direct Lt. Bye across Pennsylvania, through the Delaware Water Gap and over the Highlands Mountains toward Chatham. We came over town and made a lot noise. I was thrilled we got to buzz Chatham.

FROM THE TOP TURRET

I never heard anything from the people in town about being buzzed. They would not know who it was anyway. There were so many local men away at war. We quickly turned the plane east and flew toward the New York border.

    As I said before, we were all young kids. We didn't worry about anything. We had no fear of flying. We just didn't.

Chapter 4

THE FLYING FORTRESS & THE MIGHTY EIGHTH

It was a pretty swell machine for the time.

To climb into a B-17 Flying Fortress - to run up the engines, to move with the roar of a collective string of heavy bombers lifting off the runway, to use machinery so technologically advanced that we could drop 6,000 pounds of bombs from the air on a manufacturing plant like a sudden rain shower just blew through town, and to be part of an elite group of ten that could make her sing to the target and back - was quite an honor. It was all so new.

The B-17 Flying Fortress was the among the most modern aircraft in the U.S. inventory.

According to Boeing history, in response to the Army's request for a large, multiengine bomber, the B-17 (Model 299) prototype, financed entirely by Boeing, went from design board to flight test in less than twelve months. It was a low-winged monoplane that combined the aerodynamic features of the XB-15 giant bomber with the utilitarian features of the Model 247 transport plane. It was the first Boeing military aircraft with a flight deck, instead of an open cockpit. When the prototype took its first flight on July 28, 1935, it was the largest and heaviest plane ever built in the United States.

In reviewing the new B-17s' capacity, strength and armament a reporter from Seattle named it the Flying Fortress, a nickname that stuck.

While a few hundred were in service at the start of the War, production quickly accelerated after the United States entered combat. There was a scramble to get an adequate supply of machinery off the production line and crews trained quickly. By May 1942 the first of 3,400 new B-17s started heading off to war. The aircraft flew in every combat zone. The Flying Fortress will be best known, however, for its strategic daylight bombing of German industrial targets in the European theater.

Looking at a typical passenger airplane today it's hard to imagine that the Flying Fortress was our most advanced weapon. These warships expedited our first strategic air bombing missions.

As new planes came off the line, aviation engineers were already tweaking and adjusting design elements and advancing technologies for the next new B-17s.

We flew whatever they gave us to fly.

The Boeing B-17 was a 65,000-pound aluminum warship that was 74 feet and 9 inches long with a wingspan stretching more than 103 feet.

The four Wright Cyclone R-1820 engines had 1,200 horsepower each, enabling the plane to either cruise at 150 miles per hour or tear out of the dense black fog of flak clouds over a target at 300 miles per hour. These were nine cylinder, radial, air-cooled type engines with a 16:9 gear ratio.

Whistling up front were four sets of propellers: three-bladed Hamilton Standard propellers that were 11 feet, 7 inches in diameter. These machines could easily climb to 35,000 feet above sea level. Typically, they had a fuel capacity of 1,700 gallons and about 1,850 miles. Once the machines we flew were equipped with a Tokyo Tank we had a total capacity of 3,630 gallons and could double our range.

The firepower in a single Fortress could destroy an entire city block. Each plane was equipped with 13 50-caliber machine guns and 6,000 pounds of bombs.

Each gunner on our crew hooked up his own gun belts. I don't remember being told that there was a limit on the length of each belt, but it's been quoted that they were typically nine yards long. The gun belts came in sections and we just made them as long as we needed them to be. The size of the belts were determined by the level of opposition we anticipated. On one of our longest missions to Poland we did a lot of prep work and hooked up yards and yards of gun belts.

Once the bombs and armament were loaded into the plane there wasn't much room to move around. The flight desks were piled with grinding rows of metal. Since the space within the ball turret was so small, Fred Holt had to build shorter gun belts. Still, he managed to find places to stash yards of bullets.

The armorers carefully escorted trucks loaded with bombs to each plane and hooked them into the bomb bay through the belly of the plane, just below the wings. We were responsible for carrying our own machine guns and belts out to the plane and hooking them up. Our preflight checklist included making certain that our individual equipment was working properly.

In the turret, my gun belts loaded from the side of the machine guns and hung all the way down to the flight deck, clanking and banging against the wall of the tunnel as if they were symbols in a flight orchestra. So focused on watching the skies and eyeing my targets, I barely noticed their deafening clamor.

The Fortresses were also legendary for their ability to stay in the air after taking brutal poundings. They sometimes limped back to their bases with large chunks of the fuselage shot off.

In its 10-year production span, which halted in May 1945, some 12,726 B-17s rolled off the assembly line with varying stages of upgrades in equipment and technology. Some 4,735 planes were lost during combat missions. One of them was the Dottie J III on the first day I took her up.

Today, it's estimated that fewer than 100 airframes exist and even less are air worthy.

As a technical sergeant in the U.S. Eighth Air Force, I was the flight engineer on Crew K90 assigned to the 337th Bomb Squadron in the 96th Bomb Group, serving the Third Air Division. Our crew was part of the 45th Combat Wing that included the 96th, 388th and 452nd Bomb Groups.

All flight engineers were specially trained to have a wide knowledge of the bomber and its equipment. I was in charge of engine health monitoring. If the plane landed away from its home base, I had to be capable of repairing it and performing most jobs handled by the ground crew. As an armorer I had detailed knowledge of the aircraft's guns and bomb racks. It was critical that I maintained a working knowledge of all the aircraft's systems and, while no one thought a crash would ever happen to us, I was expected to be a key figure in any emergency landing. I was just a kid. I never expected to put all the training into place.

There were occasions when I had to crank down a wheel or check on the bomb bay door, walking along the narrow wooden planks between the bomb racks. It never occurred to me that it might be a dangerous task.

Before we took off we always had one final briefing with Lt. Bye at the plane and then followed an orderly checklist of systems to man. Each crew included two pilots, a bombardier, navigator, radio operator, and five gunners. Once Lt. Bye gave the go-ahead to run up the engines I crouched down behind the pilot and co-pilot's seat checking fuel and engine gauges. On takeoff I called off the air speeds so Lt. Bye and Lt. Malik could concentrate on keeping the airplane straight down the runway. Once we were airborne, I kept watch on the engine performance and the fuel consumption throughout the flight.

On return flights, I did the entire routine again. On the drop I read off the air speeds, so Lt. Bye knew how fast we were coming in.

To get into my position, I stepped up through a doorway just aft of the pilot's seat and climbed up a narrow passageway on the flight desk to the top turret. Imagine standing in a tube, not much wider than a large metal garbage can, with a sunroof anchored by two 50-caliber machine guns. Once I was up there, I stood through the entire mission with my feet balancing on metal footholds.

The turret was controlled by two cycle-like hand grips. The left had the gun trigger and a safety lever. The right handle worked the range finder to the sight. Pulling the handles up elevated the guns and pushing them downward brought them down. Electricity rotated the turret to the right or the left. An interruptor stopped firing the gun if it was aimed in the propeller arc or at the tail.

From the top turret I had a clear 360-degree view. I could see forever. En route to our targets, I had to diligently keep watch, looking out for enemy planes that would come up in the distance. Often they were uncomfortably close, but too far away to shoot. Enemy fighter jets would tail us in the distance, tracking our altitude and air speeds.

If I saw any enemy planes or anything unusual I'd have to call it out over the plane's radio, using the plane as a clock and noting whether the enemy was coming at us from above or below the plane. The nose was twelve o'clock. The tail was six o'clock.

I'd yell, "Three o'clock high or seven o'clock low."

Air Force pilots are always asked, which heavy bomber was better to fly: a B-17 or a B-24. There wasn't a competition between the two, not that we saw. The B-17 and the B-24 warships were the biggest American planes going at the time. We thought it was great. If you wanted to impress the military brass, however, you hoped you were assigned to a B-24. If you wanted to win the fight and go home to your family, you prayed your unit was assigned to fly B-17s. There was a reason they were called the Flying Fortress.

The B-24 warship couldn't take the punishment. It is a much larger machine that carried more firepower. I have heard it joked that the B-24 was the packing crate that the B-17 arrived in. We didn't fly too many of those out of England. Instead the B-24s were heavily used in Africa and Italy. They were used to bomb the Arab oil fields and such, because those countries didn't have much in the way of antiaircraft.

The B-17 was the primary vehicle used in the European theater. We continuously battled the onslaught of antiaircraft like swarms of gnats on a hot summer day. They arrived in front of you unexpectedly and were never welcomed. If we got a tail shot out, pieces of the plane shot out or, even an engine shot out, we could land it. It was a more dependable plane.

When we were up in the air and over a target, and they were shooting antiaircraft at us we could hear the antiaircraft going through the plane, because it was aluminum. The bullets would fly through and go out the other side. We could definitely hear it. While we were battling German fighters, three and four at a time, we could hear the antiaircraft rattling through the plane like screws in a tin can.

We were young kids, you know. We were in our glory doing what we wanted to do.

Crew K90 was part of an early model engine known as the Eighth Air Force. We were early innovators on a machine that still serves as the information operations and bomber war fighting headquarters, employing decisive global air power for the U.S. Joint Forces Command and the U.S. Strategic Command. Our history is more than 70 years old.

> The Eighth Bomber Command was activated as part of the United States Army Air Forces on January 28, 1942, at Hunter Field in Savannah, Georgia, according to the Mighty Eighth Air Force Museum. Within a month the Eighth Bomber Command joined its parent unit, Eighth Air Force, and under the leadership of Brigadier General Ira C. Eaker, established a permanent home on English soil

to prepare for its mission of conducting aerial bombardment missions against Nazi-occupied Europe.

From May 1942 to July 1945, the Eighth Bomber Command planned and executed the American daylight precision and strategic bombing campaigns over Nazi-occupied Europe from a former girls school in High Wycombe, England.

During the war, the Eighth Air Force became the greatest air armada in history. By early 1944, the Army recognized its Air Forces in Europe. As part of a redesignation detail the Eighth Air Force became the United States Strategic Air Forces in Europe and the Eighth Bomber Command became the Eighth Air Force. The Eighth Air Force reached a total strength of more than 200,000 people by June 1944. It is estimated that more then 350,000 Americans served in the Eighth Air Force during World War II.

At its peak, the Eighth Air Force could dispatch more than 2,000 four-engine bombers and more than 1,000 fighters on a single mission. For these reasons, the command of the Eighth Air Force became known as "The Mighty Eighth."

The Mighty Eighth compiled an impressive record in the war. This achievement, however, carried a high price. Half of the U.S. Army Air Force's casualties were suffered by Eighth Air Force members (more than 47,000 casualties, with more than 26,000 dead).

Seventeen Medals of Honor went to Eighth Air Force personnel during the war. They had been awarded a number of other medals by war's end, including 220 Distinguished Service Crosses and 442,000 Air Medals. Many more awards were made to Eighth Air Force veterans after the war that remain uncounted. There were 261 fighter aces in the Mighty Eighth during the war, including 31 aces that had 15 or more aircraft kills apiece. Another 305 enlisted gunners were also recognized as aces.

Each time I read those casualty numbers, however, I am reminded just how lucky I was to come home to Chatham.

Gerard J. Caporaso,
U.S. Army Air Force 1942.

Military gear lined up on cots outside the new barracks at
Amarillo Field, Amarillo, Texas on Nov. 9, 1942.

(Above) New barracks and dirt pathways show an airbase still under construction at Amarillo Field, Amarillo, Texas on Nov. 9, 1942. (Left) Gerard Caporaso with Mrs. F. Polter and her daughter Gail, who hosted several Air Force soldiers for Thanksgiving dinner at her home in Amarillo, Texas in November 1942.

Gerard Caporaso standing outside barracks at Amarillo Field, Amarillo, Texas in 1942.

Gerard Caporaso on horseback on top of a mountain in Palo Duro Canyon State Park, Texas on January 4, 1943.

(Above) Gerard Caporaso (far right) with (from left) Warren Caldwell, E. Carnivale, and Denis Carey in Palo Duro Canyon State Park, Texas where they discovered a wild hog while riding horseback on January 4, 1943.

(Left) Victor Carozzo, Gerard Caporaso and Warren Caldwell celebrating on furlough in El Paso, Texas on April 21, 1943.

(Right) Gerard Caporaso (far left) with E. Carnivale, McIntyre, Warren Caldwell and Burrows at the Boeing facility in Seattle, Washington where they were sent for training on B-17 bombers on Feb 7, 1943. (Below) Gerard J. Caporaso on base. Photo provided from the private collection of Brigid Bye O'Donnell and reproduced with permission.

Crew K90 in Iceland in August 1943. Gerard Caporaso is pictured in the back row, second from the right. Photo provided from the private collection of Brigid Bye O'Donnell and reproduced with permission.

Lt. Raymond F. Bye, U.S. Army Air Force, 1942. Photos provided from the private collection of Brigid Bye O'Donnell and reproduced with permission.

Crew K90 group photo - Gerard Caporaso in pictured on the left in the back row. Photo: provided from the private collection of Brigid Bye O'Donnell and reproduced with permission.

A B-17 bomber in flight during World War II.

Chapter 5

THE CROSSING

There wasn't much discussion. No elaborate goodbyes. No emotional separations. We were going war. Before we arrived we had already seen the world.

We left the arid dry dustbowl of the northern Texas Panhandle, flew north to Lambert Field in St. Louis, enjoyed the view of amber waves of grain in the Midwest and the lush marbled green mountains that blanketed the Northeast, especially over Pennsylvania and New Jersey in mid summer, and kissed the coast of Staten Island. We landed on bases in Bangor, Maine; Goose Bay, Labrador; Reykjavik, Iceland; and Prestwick, Scotland, before being shuttled to England and put on a train.

It was a long squiggly s-curve of a trip that took us nearly half way around the world: more than 5,300 air miles. We went from the heat of summer to ice and snow. The further away we traveled from home the closer to war we came.

I was still satisfied that I made my mark on Chatham, buzzing the treetops and making enough noise over town to snap my neighbors' attention away from their daily routines. I wonder what my mother and father would have thought of all of that. Would they have liked knowing their son was just above them, covering the skies, and serving his duty or would I have been scolded for making too much noise in the machine? I never knew.

As with all the air fields we trained on or passed through, Lambert Field in St. Louis was a whirl of commotion when we arrived in the summer of 1943. St. Louis' industry became an aviation manufacturing base during the War. The region was expanding to fulfill an order for 3,000 new planes. This is where they rolled off the line. We didn't stay long. While arrangements were being made for our crossing we had a few days off. One buddy of mine, the tail gunner Alton Baer was always ready to go. He always found a way to sneak off base at night and I managed to follow him.

Our shiny new B-17 was waiting for us on the hardstand. We dropped off the old B-17 we flew there and then went for instructions on the small technical adjustments made on the new plane. We called her ours. We were as trained and as ready as we could be. This was our first stop in the crossing. Now we were mentally ready to go fight the enemy and protect our country in a brand new B-17 with all the latest technological advancements. When you're flying a Fortress, that's an extremely powerful feeling. We were 20-somethings who thought we were invincible.

In democratic fashion, we all agreed on the name The Outhouse Mouse that Lt. Bye wanted for the plane. He had someone design the nose art of a mouse peaking around the corner of an outhouse and carried it in his pocket over to Scotland.

After swirling over Chatham and New York we stopped to refuel in Bangor, Maine and then landed overnight in Goose Bay, Labrador in Newfoundland.

> Goose Bay, now known as Canadian Forces Base Goose Bay, was built by the Canadian Government as part of its contribution to the war effort. It was used as a refueling and shuttle stop for overseas flights by the United States and Great Britain. With three 7,000-foot paved runways it was the largest airport in the world when we landed there for an overnight stay.

In the morning we took off over Labrador Sea, crossed the southern tip of Greenland and flew more than 1,500 miles to Reykjavik, Iceland. We were air over water for about six hours.

When we got to Reykjavik-Keflavik Airport, our commanding officers gave each gunner 50 machine gun shells, just in case the Germans came over. Sometimes they flew over Scotland, but we never had to shoot them.

THE CROSSING

The airport was built by the United States military during World War II. The U.S. Army Air Forces needed an airfield that was capable of operating heavy bombers and providing fighter airstrips. The two runways of the fighter field, known as Meeks Field, had just been christened as part of Operation Bolero when we arrived. We were among the first wave of transatlantic military flights to land there.

> Operation Bolero was the code name used to reference the United Kingdom in the strategic air force buildup in preparation for the initial cross-channel invasion plan known as Operation Roundup. Slated for April 1943, the Roundup called for the transporting and housing of one million U.S. troops: 525,000 ground troops, 240,000 Air Force troops and 235,000 from Services of Supply. Crew K90 was part of the basing of 69 combat groups and their service units, including 21 heavy bomb groups (B-17 and B-24 fighters), eight medium bomb groups (B-26 and B-25), nine light bomb groups (A-20), 17 fighter groups, six observation groups and eight transport groups.

In Iceland we were frozen in for a couple of days. It snowed like heck for almost a week and we couldn't take off. It was there that we first encountered people opposed to our participation in the war. After settling into the base, we went to town and pulled into a restaurant. People there weren't happy to see us. They served us - took care of us - but we certainly knew we weren't welcomed.

The Icelandic government had received many requests from the British government to consent to the occupation, but it always declined on the basis of the Neutrality Policy. Throughout the war the British and American soldiers built bases in Reykjavik, boosted the local economy right out of the Great Depression era and multiplied its population. At some point there were as many soldiers in Reykjavik as there were residents. I suppose they enjoyed the security that an influx of thousands of British and American soldiers provided. They certainly enjoyed the benefits of money being invested and spent in the country. Still, the locals didn't like being a bullseye for enemy fighters. We were critically necessary, but unwelcome tourists.

The thing I remember the most about our time there was that we were able to buy cigarettes at 50-cents a carton. Most of us didn't have much money to buy anything, but we bought a couple of cartoons.

Letter home - USO Letterhead
Somewhere over Iceland August 27, 1943
Dear Mom,
I know you won't get this letter for a week or more. I thought I'd write again. I am feeling swell and everything is OK. I hope everyone home is fine. I have often read about these places, but I never thought I'd see them. By the time you get this letter I will be gone from here. Don't worry about me, because everything will be all right. How is Betty? Tell her to be a good girl until I get home. You can start writing to the letter on the outside of this envelope. Please write soon. There isn't much else I can say. So I will have to close. Give my regards to everyone.
Love Jerry.

The trip to Prestwick, Scotland took us 840 or so miles over water. After training on land for almost a year, we really got a bird's eye view of what it was like to be a seagull. The approach to Scotland took us over a series of smaller islands and outcroppings of land, over the Firth of Clyde and onto the L-shaped runway of Prestwick Airport, now the Glasgow Prestwick International Airport.

We got to take a couple of days off. Naturally, as young men do, we headed into town to check things out. If we were lucky we'd find a dance hall. It was there I got to see my first indoor ice skating rink. It was neat. The complex also had a roller skating rink, which was good, because most of us could roller skate, but not ice skate.

Our crew was split up for a bit in Prestwick. We were divided up into groups. The radio operators were sent to different spots. Armorers went for further ballistics training to prepare them for different environments and varying weather. Lt. Bye and Lt. Malik had pilot business. The other engineer and I were shipped down to The Wash in England for further training and refresher courses. The Wash is a square-mouthed bay and estuary on the eastern coast of England where Norfolk meets Lincolnshire. The conditions were good there for rehearsing flight training and maneuvers over The Wash and the North Sea. We were briefed there on different aspects of the planned bombing raids.

When we got out of our training, about a week to 10 days later, we were informed that we were heading to our base. We didn't know where we were going. They just told us to get on a train.

Our B-17 - the one we thought would be our steady plane, The Outhouse Mouse we named and planned nose art for, the nice new shiny one with all the

THE CROSSING

new stuff in it - was taken away. We never saw it again. I'll never know if our plane was the famed flying ace of the same name.

If they told us the name of our base in England, no one remembered.

I asked, "How will I know where to get off?"

"Don't worry. The conductor will tell you when to get off. Just tell him Eccles Road. Get off at the station and a man there will tell you where to go," our instructor said, handing us our tickets. So we did. We landed in a small train station that was probably the one in Diss. From the platform we could see nothing in the distance, except a tower. Certainly there had to be a mistake. We asked a station engineer where the Air Force field was. The guy told us to walk up the street about a mile and we'll see the gates on the right hand side. That was as much as we knew about the base. Sure enough, ten minutes later we were standing at the foot of two large metal gates. Our entire crew reconnected at the base in staggered arrivals.

I didn't know the name of the base was Snetterton Heath for years. Decades later I was working in the Chatham Post Office when a customer - another Air Force veteran - was talking to a few fellas about his base in England. He mentioned Eccles Road and I knew instantly that we served on the same base. The other guys said, "Eccles Road? What were you doing?" He said he was put in charge of watching the coal. There were giant mounds of coal that people would steal. He said he didn't know if people would steal it or not. If they did, they only really took a few buckets full.

> Snetterton Heath airfield was located six miles south west of Attleborough in Norfolk, England. It was home base for the 96th Bombardment Group of heavy bombers and the medium bombers of the 386th Bombardment Group. The airfield had one main 6,000-foot runway with two secondary runways of 4,200 feet each. Together they created a perfect triangle, providing pilots three directions to land: north to south, east to west and southwest to northeast on the main runway. There were four T-2 hangars. With the arrival of the Eighth Air Force armada, the hardstands were quickly expanded to 50 on the southern and eastern sides of the airfield. Access from A11, London Road, the main road in between Norwich and New Market, was restricted.
>
> Hardstands are the paved areas used for parking heavy vehicles and bombers. The paving material is generally thicker and more durable than pavement used in constructing driveways and city streets. We

couldn't have B-17s sinking into the drippy English mud. Sometimes these hardstands were constructed of the frying pan type with 10-foot sections of galvanized steel pressed into compacted dirt.

Once we crossed through the front gates we didn't know where we were going. An official finally took us to an assigned Quonset hut and told us to settle in. The recalcitrant realities of war welcomed us. As we looked around we could tell the private possessions of two or three crews were neatly hung among wooden bunk beds and foot lockers throughout the hut. The official told us they had a bombing raid that day and a crew didn't return. As such, new space suddenly became available for us. In the moment we tried to quickly process the news - a crew didn't return - as he simply said, "This is where you are going to stay."

We didn't realize it at the time, but returning crews on base frequently helped themselves to the Army gear and possessions of crew members, who were shot down.

We non-coms lived in a cluster of dozens of Quonset huts in the southern end of the base, near the firing range and the aviation fuel storage. The commissioned officers slept in built barracks in the southeastern corner of the base.

> Quonset huts were half-moon shaped prefabricated structures of corrugated galvanized steel that were widely used during the war as multi purpose light weight buildings that could be shipped anywhere and assembled without skilled labor. The original designs were about 16 feet wide and 36 feet long. The sides were made of steel and the ends were covered with plywood. These structures were used as barracks, briefing rooms, training rooms, medical offices, latrines, housing and bakeries. It's estimated that more than 150,000 Quonset huts were manufactured by the United States during World War II.

The first combat crews began arriving at Snetterton Heath in June 1943 from the Royal Air Force's Andrews Field. To help facilitate control among the thousands of bombers arriving in England, the U.S. Army Air Force devised a system of aircraft tail markings to identify groups and wings. Both the Eighth and Fifteenth Air Forces used a system of large, readily identifiable geometric symbols combined with numbers or letters to designate groups. Our 96th Group

THE CROSSING

tail code was a square with a C in the middle. We were still among the first crews to arrive when we organized at the base some six weeks later.

> Letter home - September 20, 1943
> *Dear Mom,*
> *I just received two letters from you. I was certainly glad to get them. One was to Scott Field (Mo.). It was one month old. The other was a U-letter dated just two weeks ago. It was still good to get them no matter how old they are. I got one package with two boxes of gum when I was in Scott Field, but I didn't get the other package yet. It will probably get to me one of these days. Send me some candy, something like Baby Ruths, Milky Ways or Hershey bars. We can't get them here. Don't forget to send me the Chatham Press. I'm feeling fine and everything is OK here. We started flying again. We're still going to school, but I haven't had a pass yet. I sent $250 home by radio from my last camp in England. Did you get it? And did you get the package from Texas, yet? (There was a gift for my baby sister Betty in it.) I hope so, because there were some pictures of my crew in it. How is everything back home? How is Butch? Give him a kiss for me. How are the kids back home? Tell them to write. That's about all for now. So I'll close. Give everyone a kiss for me.*
> *Love, Jerry*
> *T/Sgt. Gerard J. Caporaso 32461208*
> *96th Bomb Group (H)*
> *337th Sqdn. APO#634*
> *c/o Postmaster New York City, N.Y.*

The pilot and I were given brand new bicycles so we could cycle out to the plane in preparation for the preflight of missions. The rest of the crew had to scrounge around for a bike, maybe one from a crew that didn't return, or hop on a truck to get out to the plane.

We were treated well at Snetterton Heath. While we were there we had these young girls from town, who would come in to do our wash. We had to pay for it, but they didn't charge too much. I always gave them a little extra, some cigarettes and chocolate bars - D bars, the thick dark chocolate kind. They enjoyed them very much. Cigarettes and chocolate were so scarce during the war. Their parents could trade them.

We never got to go into town, but we were granted one weekend-long pass to go to London. Someone rode us down to the station and we took a train through Cambridge to London.

When we weren't flying we still worked a highly scheduled day. We got up early for breakfast and calisthenics, the usual stuff of jumping jacks, pushups and running. Afterward there might be further training sessions or work to do around the base.

One of my favorite memories of our crew is that we used to play cards together. We were very good, too. I still chuckle thinking about that day in England when we were hunkered down under the plane, waiting for something to happen. We had nothing to do and a set of dice in our hands. As time lingered we started a dice game. Since we weren't familiar with the currency, we ended up betting English pound notes, which were worth four American dollars, and five-pound notes worth $20. The game got more exciting as the day wore on, especially for me. I closed out the night with $600 in my pocket.

We had a good crew and always played together.

Chapter 6

THE THEATER

Official records of the United States Air Force credit our crew as having flown eight missions. By my count we flew ten, including two missions aborted while we were en route to the target.

I always counted those other two missions, because we were on duty all day from the moment our feet hit the floor next to our bunks for a pre-dawn briefing.

Once we were stationed on base we didn't have time to dwell on our life, combat missions or our mortality. We just didn't think too much of it back then. When we had a mission we went to the briefing, got into the plane, got into our positions and took off. Our crew had a bit role in the strategic cog to overwhelm the German war machine. I'm satisfied that we did our job professionally by hitting our targets and downing a few planes, even on the last mission.

You have to remember that the United States got into the war late, December 1941. By 1942 the country was preparing to get the Air Force and Army ready. My crew didn't get over there until 1943. It wasn't that we didn't want to, but we weren't there yet. The English were being decimated in daylight bombing raids. They were losing too many planes and were devastated by many casualties. So they took to night raids, which were safer, but strategically ineffective. The U.S. Army Air Force, as it was known then, took over the daylight bombing raids to Germany and the European Theater in 1943. We were trained to fly either way, day or night. Our instructions were a constant rote drilling: Be prepared.

FROM THE TOP TURRET

We were one of the first groups of the Eighth Air Force to arrive in England. While we landed in mid-August at Snetterton Heath it took awhile to get it together.

To understand the three Air Divisions that constitute the Eighth Air Force think of a large oak tree with three big branches reaching out from the base of the trunk: The First Air Division, Second Air Division, and Third Air Division. Off each branch, are maybe a half dozen other stronger branches called combat wings and fighter groups. From there are smaller branches called bomb squadrons. Now let's climb back up that tree. I served on the 337th Bombardment Squadron in the 96th Bomb Group. It was one of three bomb groups that composed the 45th Bomb Wing in the Third Air Division of the Eighth Air Force. It was served entirely by B-17 heavy bombers.

> The 96th Bomb Group entered combat in May 1943, just before Crew K90 arrived at Snetterton Heath with the 337th Bombardment Squadron, and functioned primarily as a strategic bombardment organization under the Eighth Air Force. What looked initially like a series of random unconnected attacks on factories and installations had a discerning affect on the war. In the daylight bombing raids, the Eighth Air Force championed attacks on the German industrial engines: the shipyards, harbors, railway yards, aerodromes, oil refineries, air fields, aircraft factories and other industrial targets in Germany, France, Holland, Belgium, Norway, Poland, Hungary and Czechoslovakia. Additionally, the 96th attacked coastal defenses such as railway bridges, gun emplacements, and field batteries. German fighter planes weren't rolling off the line if the factories that engineered their parts were destroyed.
>
> Most conveniently reached from the Third Air Division headquarters, Snetterton Heath units often led to major operations carrying commanding generals.

I wish I still had my little address book, the one I kept in my footlocker in the Quonset hut on base. It was a little leather-bound number I brought with me. After each mission, I recorded everything I remembered: where we went, how we flew, and the targets we hit. I wanted to document my missions, my history. We weren't allowed to bring anything personal with us on the plane, however.

THE THEATER

After my last mission, all my private possessions back at the base, including a ring given to me by my parents and my rosary beads, disappeared. As much as I still remember, with flashbacks rekindling the moments, smells, and emotions of everything we did, the perfect outline detailing my missions is somewhat sketchy after 70 years. Yet, the crew is still vivid to me. I can still see us climbing up into our positions and going through a preflight checklist.

Our routines on base were steeped in military structure. Each day we rose early and went to a hearty breakfast of eggs, bacon, toast, juice and coffee, never powdered eggs. The Air Force ate well. On days we weren't flying we headed off to a nearby field for calisthenics where we fluidly shifted between building strength and flexibility and endurance training.

When the all-go sign for a mission came down from headquarters we were awakened at 4 a.m., while the night was still black and eerie. We'd head straight to breakfast. Afterward we walked as a group across the base to the briefing room.

In many World War II accounts it has been noted that only the pilot and navigator attended the morning briefing meetings and then informed the rest of the crew. That wasn't the case with us. There weren't that many fighter groups in England yet. Because we were serving early in the war, we all attended the briefings. The room was readied with several hundred chairs organized in a long rectangle and a platform at the front where several chairs anchored either side of a wall-size bulletin board. A few crude spotlights hung from the ceiling off long extension cords, facing the wall. They were the kind of lights you use around your house when you're fixing stuff. The bulletin board was always covered with a large sheet when we arrived at the briefing. A very large American flag draped from the front wall. Our country's colors remained in our view. There would be a rumble of nervous pent-up conversation in the room. Of course we always wondered where we were going. Our crew couldn't wait to fly to Germany. We settled down instantly as the leaders walked into the room and with very dramatic style, tore the sheet off the wall while saying, "Here is your target for today."

We never knew where we were going until we were briefed. There were no surprises once we boarded the plane, however. We knew where we were going. We knew what was expected in terms of weather, terrain, opposition, strategy and targets. We just didn't know what we would see, or what would happen to us. It was war, of course. We knew there was German opposition to our very existence. That was the emotional load we carried.

Of course, we didn't know what was heavy opposition and what was light, until we started flying. Every mission was an exciting mission, because we were heading toward bombing Germany. We couldn't help, but get excited.

After briefing meetings the pilot and I headed to the hardstand for a preflight check of the plane we were assigned. I rode the bicycle over. Since we always flew a different base plane on every mission, we had to be as diligent as a forensic scientist with these inspections. I had to ensure that the fuel tanks were filled and the filler caps secured. We had to check all the equipment on the plane, assess the bombs that were being loaded into racks in the bomb bay and inspect the plane for any damage that the ground crew might have missed. Anything noted I reported to Lt. Bye. There wasn't much I found. We had good ground crews at Snetterton Heath. After my preflight inspection, I cleaned and installed the turret guns. The machines guns and steel belts were loaded last as the crew arrived in Jeeps or 4 by 4 trucks.

Burning out machine guns was one of the technical problems that we often addressed. It was easy to burn out the barrels. We had machine gun triggers. We were supposed to shoot them in short bursts. Once we were still over target, we generally dropped bombs for 15 to 30 minutes. The ensuing enemy fight, however, could last another 30 minutes to an hour or more. Those short bursts then became a prolonged body-rattling charge. You never wanted to burn out a barrel, but it happened. We always had to inform the ground crew upon returning if we had long bursts. Sometimes we had spare barrels with us on the plane that we could replace in the guns. Mine never jammed. I always took care of my machine guns.

The gun belts were created before each flight. Our mission determined the length of the belts, since we hooked several together. Woven among the steel 50-caliber strings were tracer bullets, which were 50-caliber shells with gunpowder that just burned. They showed us where we were shooting. I could see the tracers in the planes. At first they told us not to put the tracer bullets any closer than every fifth bullet on the gun belt, because the Germans would follow the bullets. Later on we started putting them further apart, maybe every seven to 10 bullets away.

THE THEATER

Before we took off Lt. Bye held one last casual briefing outside the plane, reviewing our instructions, the anticipated length of the mission, eyes on target and reminding us to keep alert. It was a very friendly thing. Then we took our positions in the plane.

I climbed into the side door with Lt. Bye and Lt. Malik and took my spot behind the pilots' seats, readied to read off air speeds. The navigator Meryl Woodside and the bombardier Bill Kieran took their posts in the nose of the plane. The radio operator Kenneth Nice was halfway back in the flight deck. Charles Gattman and Mike Olynik, the waist gunners, were on the side of the plane and the tail gunner Alton Baer Jr. was in back. Fred Holt took his spot in the ball turret. On takeoff Charles and Mike usually sat on the floor of the radio room. Alton and Fred often went straight into their positions, because they were difficult to get to. Sometimes, they also sat in the radio room.

There was one tradition we had before takeoffs. Once the bomb bay was loaded, we wrote something for Adolf Hitler on each of the bombs. They weren't nice words: the F word and stuff. I don't think they found too many of them, but I'm sure occasionally some of the bombs didn't explode and people found them.

Most of the time the 96th Bomb Group didn't have enough planes to make up the formation on its own. Instead we flew with the 100th Bombardment Group out of Thorpe Abbots airfield, about 20 miles southwest of Norwich, or the 388th Bombardment Group, based about six miles southeast of Thetford in Suffolk at RAF Knettishall. We flew together. If they didn't have enough planes to form a formation then we did. Likewise, if we didn't have enough planes then they did.

The Flying Fortress was a beautiful machine. It was the Model T Ford of the airways. We thought it was great. Every time a new one came off the line, something was updated in it. For the most part, however, we flew the older model olive green planes in England, not the silver ones. The planes we flew had flexible guns in the nose and tail. They sure were beat up. We made the best of it though.

When newer models arrived they were outfitted with turrets in the nose and tail. They were silver and nose art became wildly trendy.

Until we were over target we were always on watch for anything that would cause trouble, anything seen on land over enemy territory or anything in the sky. Always. After we left England and were over the English Channel, we had to test our guns. We often tested them with short bursts over Denmark. We figured if the Germans were down there we might get one of them.

We had to be alert for German fighter planes. In 1943 the German Luftwaffe was in its prime. They caused a lot of trouble. Sometimes the Americans had escorts fighter planes, P-51 Mustangs, on missions. Early escort planes didn't have the fuel tank capacity to fly an entire mission. Eventually they were outfitted with a wing tank so they could endure longer trips. The escorts traveled as far as they could and then wiggled a wing to sign off before heading back to base. We never had a fighter escort with us. If they were on our missions they were escorting another formation.

Our official missions included an airfield in France; Rheims, France; Emden, Germany; Saarbrucken, Germany; Bremen, Germany; Gdynia, Poland; Munster, Germany; and the war's single most important raid on a ball bearing factory in Schweinfurt, Germany. My incomplete, but definitely flown missions include a submarine pen in France and an attempt to target the famed German battle ship, the Scharnhorst, in Norway.

We never flew the same plane twice. Each time we took off in an available base plane, because the previous plane we flew came back pretty well shot up.

We bombed the runways, the factories and the planes. The first few air raids they sent us on were called milk runs, because they weren't expected to be challenging. Yet, we still had life-threatening opposition. My first air raid was at an air field in southern France, shortly after we arrived in England on August 31, 1943. Our mission was to wreck the air field, the planes, and the runways a bit so they couldn't fly anymore. At least for a while until they rebuilt it. I don't remember where it was exactly, but we did take down the planes. The 96th was flying missions to Merville, Abbeville-Poix, Conches Evreaux, Bourdeaux, and Watten in France around that time. We were somewhere in the mix.

We fought a lot of opposition on our missions, because of the antiaircraft on the ground. On every raid we spotted a German ME110 twin engine plane flying off our wing to our coast, giving exact directions on our altitude and air speed to the anti aircraft down below. That's why the antiaircraft was so accurate. They were getting information from their own people. We couldn't shoot them down, because they were too far away. We were shot up badly on every raid.

After several bombing missions we were eager to go to Germany. No one on the crew had been. We didn't substitute out individual crew members to fill in with another crew. As such, we were all waiting to go. That was the plumb assignment.

The first time we entered into Germany it was a big deal. In the briefing room our commander tore the sheet from the wall map and simply said, "Well, today you're going to see through Germany." That was a big thing. That's when we targeted the shipyards in Emden in late September.

We knew it was something different. We knew we were killing and trying to end the war, you know. We were trying to destroy their industry. That's what we were after: the ports, trains, factories, and marshaling yards. We knew it was going to be tough and it was. The Germans had plenty of antiaircraft all around their targets. We were lucky we didn't get shot down before Schweinfurt. We knew what we were over there for and we were doing it. As such, we were always excited going into Germany. Hitler was our enemy and so was Germany.

The longest bombing raid was a rambling 12-hour round trip to attack the ports in Gdynia, Poland on October 9, 1943. Once we took off we had to create our formations, joining squadrons from the 100th and 338th. It was the better part of a day. A formation entailed three groups of seven planes flying in three triangles, like migrating birds. Seven flew high. Seven took the center and seven flew low. We flew over the English Channel and the North Sea, crossed Denmark and turned southeast toward Poland.

We were cruising at a lower altitude over water most of the time. It was interesting. I could see the landscape. We weren't flying that high over the English Channel or the North Sea. I was keeping watch in the top turret, just glancing around. We saw a couple of enemy planes come up after us going over the North Sea. They didn't stay too long, because we had too much fire power. Over Denmark we were still low. Normally we flew at 25,000 feet on bombing raids, but we were down below that. As a matter of fact, I don't think we even had oxygen masks on until later when we got closer to our target and reached the right pickle-barrel bombing altitude of 20,000 to 25,000 feet. We had to wear the masks at 10,000 feet. It wasn't a problem.

It was cold up there though. The frostbite risk was high, especially for the waist gunners. Inside the plane we wore bunny suits to stay warm. They were extra large flight suits with giant slippers that plugged in like an electric blanket to keep us warm. They were a cumbersome number that was difficult to walk in, because they didn't have real soles. I wore mine briefly, but as we got closer to a target I took it off. The top turret rotated and, as such, I couldn't keep the suit plugged in and work. Instead I just wore extra clothing - anything I had - and gloves.

Most of the time we were just standing and looking out the windows. I was in the top turret just glancing around. It was my job to watch for planes coming overheard. I was to inform the first of the crew, which direction the planes were coming from. Two o'clock high or two o'clock low. Seven enemies, three o'clock high. The ball turret gunner also notified us of planes coming up from down below. I had to be alert at all times, because I never knew when fighter planes were coming in or from where they were coming. In all our raids we always flew different flights and altitudes. Never the same.

Communicating wasn't hard to do once we were airborne, because we were hooked up to the aircraft interphone. All we had to do was press the button and speak. Generally we didn't talk unless we had something to report. I liked that about our crew. We had an amiable rhythm of working together all the time. No hot shots.

We met heavy opposition from antiaircraft and fighter planes in Gdynia. When those things burst in the sky it would be completely black in front of you. Flak was exploding all around us in waves of randomness that increased over time. I could taste the blackened gun powder in the air, a dry stale metallic mixture I inhaled with the salty sweat beading on my face. The only way we could avoid a complete invasion was to track where they were imploding. Lt. Bye would turn toward the one that just exploded, because the enemy needed a few minutes to reload antiaircraft. We'd swerve just to avoid it. There was no place you could really go. We were flying so fast.

Enemy fighters were coming at us from one direction at a few hundred miles an hour. We'd dodge that pile of flak and suddenly swerve to avoid another group of enemy fighters coming at us from another direction at a few hundred miles an hour. We were shot at pretty badly. We had to be careful not to let the flak break up our formations. Many times I just shot in front of them and kept shooting so that the enemy fighters would fly into my bursts. I just had to keep my guns in front of me. It was like moving through a swarm of deadly gnats.

It was an exciting time. We all wanted to fly. It was good to be in a position where we could shoot at enemy planes. The two turrets, the top and the ball turret, were the prime places for locating approaching enemy planes. I was glad for my post.

After the Gdynia raid, Lt. Bye took a photograph of the entire crew and had us each sign the photo. We were already worn and haggard. I vaguely remembered it when Lt. Bye's daughter, Brigid O'Donnell, showed it to me during a reunion in the course of writing this book.

Our one steady tradition in the Air Force was to make certain our short snorters were always in our wallets, especially when we hit the canteen after a raid. A short snorter is a banknote signed by people traveling together on an aircraft. What started as a tradition with Alaskan bush flyers in the 1920s quickly spread to the military. During the war, we all kept a single dollar bill signed by each crew member as a keepsake of our travels together. If we didn't have our short snorter with us when we went to the bar, we might just get stuck paying the bar bill for everyone. That was the game. Never leave a Quonset hut without it.

We attacked the manufacturing harbors and big cities on the Rhein River. One of our missions to a harbor was heavy with antiaircraft. Despite all the training, you really don't know what heavy opposition feels like until it's all coming at you with deadly force. Every second you move could either save your life or end it. You are so focused on the moment that you can't feel the sweat streaming down your spine and pooling in your boots or your heart pounding like a bass drum on the outside of your chest. So often I would be charging enemy fighters in the turret and hear antiaircraft blowing through one side of the airplane and exiting the other. As mighty as the Fortress was, it was still a big metal plane.

FROM THE TOP TURRET

One of our most notorious missions was to attack a harbor on the coast of France where the Germans had submarine pens they used to store and repair subs and other boats. We needed extra firepower. In preparation for the flight, the ground crew installed 2000-pound bombs under each wing that were supposed to release electronically. We had to arm the things before we took off, because we couldn't arm them in flight in the same way the bombardier pulled pins from bombs in the bomb bay. We couldn't get out there to do that. On takeoff, we flew up and over the English Channel when we started having engine trouble. We couldn't quite make it to France and had to abort. So, we turned back around. The pilot landed back in Snetterton Heath with those bombs on the wings. Well, he sure got chewed out for that.

If they had fallen off we would have blown the whole place up. A standard 500-pound bomb for a precision mission had a lethal radius of 60 to 90 feet and dug a crater two feet deep and nine feet wide. The pilot said, "Well, I was saving a couple of bombs." He was told, "You don't save a couple of bombs and blow up an air base." I count it as a mission too, because we got up and over the English Channel. That's the only bad thing I could say about Lt. Bye in all his missions. It wasn't bad to me, because I figured he was saving the bombs, too. It says a lot about the steel strength and focus of Lt. Bye's abilities. Without a moment's waiver, I was ready to get back on a plane with him.

After that we were sent up to Bergen, Norway in an attempt to attack the Scharnhorst battleship. When we heard we were going there we were very excited at the chance of sinking a battleship, a big one. We had to fly over the English Channel, up toward Norway. We got three quarters of the way there when they aborted the raid. Apparently, the ship had taken off sometime during the night. If we had gotten there to drop our bombs we would have had all kinds of reconnaissance photos. Boy, did we look forward to that. It was our big chance to sink a big German battleship. I still do count that trip as a mission.

> The Scharnhorst was a capital ship, often described as a battlecruiser, of the German Kriegsmarine. She was a lead ship of her class. Completed in 1939, the ship was armed with a main battery of nine 11-inch C/34 guns in three triple turrets. In early 1942, after repeated British bombing raids, the Scharnhorst and the Gneisenau made a daylight run up the English Channel from occupied France to Germany. In early 1943, the Scharnhorst joined the Bismark class battleship Tirpitz in Norway to destroy Allied convoys to the Soviet Union. The Scharnhorst and several

destroyers sortied from Norway to attack a convoy when they were instead intercepted by British navel patrols. During the Battle of North Cape, the Royal Navy battleship HMS Duke of York sank the Scharnhorst. Only 36 of the 1,968 member crew were pulled from the icy seas.

Returning to base was a grateful, but bittersweet experience. We rallied on the descent over a vast patchwork of English farm fields once we eyed the three runways of Snetterton Heath. While we hobbled home, often looking like olive green Swiss cheese with a tail off or a wing shot up, we knew others weren't returning. There were no cheering sections of ground crews waving flags at us. We were just doing our job. We unhooked our machine guns and carried out any gear. The ground crew immediately took over to assess the damage.

After a mission we were expected to be ready to fly again the next day, but we never did. We always had a day or two off, sometimes a week, but we flew often.

The Air Force was a completely different life. That's what I liked about it. When we got back from a raid we lived well. Someone always offered us a shot. I didn't take it, but some of the guys did. There would be a meal waiting for us or table of Spam sandwiches. Some crews took food and coffee with them on flights, but we didn't. In the morning after a raid we ate bacon and eggs for breakfast. We always ate good food. It was completely different from the ground soldiers, who ate rations.

There was a big difference in the culture between air and ground troops. We had moments of being off duty back at the base. A ground troop never did.

Ground solders were shooting at someone and shooting to protect themselves, too. While we had no real fear, we did realize there were several ways of losing our lives. I never actually shot directly at someone. I never saw myself look into the eyes of the enemy - one person - up in the air and kill them. I saw bombs hit their targets. I saw my bullets go through airplanes. I saw planes we shot go down. I knew we killed people when their planes crashed, but I never saw myself put a bullet directly into somebody. I'll never know. Maybe I just hit their engines. With 10 gunners on the plane we really couldn't tell anyway.

When we were shooting directly at an enemy fighter plane, all kinds of bullets were being jack hammered at it. We were in a formation. Seven or eight planes of crew members were shooting at one fighter. We never actually knew who shot them down. Many pilots claimed that they shot a plane down, but they could never really know.

It was quite a different war than what the ground soldiers were put through. They had a tougher time. We dropped bombs on people. Ground crews were actually shooting at people. Comparing the two extremes, the Air Force was always gravy.

Until we got shot down, of course.

> Letter Home - Sept. 24, 1943
> Somewhere in England
> *Dear Mom,*
> *I received a letter from you yesterday from Scott Field that was dated a month ago. Even though it was old I was still glad to get it. I am feeling fine and everything is OK here. We should be getting a pass pretty soon. I haven't had one since we got here. How is everyone at home. How is Butch (our nickname for my baby sister Betty)? I hope she is a good girl. How are the kids making out at school? There is a newspaper clipping in this letter. Save it for me. I will be sending quite a few from now on. So save them all for me. I hope you received all the letters from me so far. I hope you got the package from Texas yet. Well Mom, that's about all for now. So I'll close. Give my regards to everybody.*
> *Love, Jerry.*

Chapter 7

BLACK THURSDAY

We had no way of knowing what lay ahead for us.

In the previous week, we had flown three consecutive air raids: the ports and warehouses in Bremen, Germany on October 8, a 12-hour bomb run against the shipyards in Gdynia, Poland on October 9, and an attack on a military base in Munster, Germany on the 10th that targeted a munitions factory producing sulphur mustard gas and the new nerve agent, GA. It was a deadly week of beautifully crisp, clear fall afternoons. What became known as Black Week was about to see its final mission.

At 4 a.m. on Thursday we were awakened from the deepest sleep in our hut and ordered to get ready to mount a maximum effort. In the middle of the dark English woodlands, we washed and dressed quickly, hurried off to the mess for a quick breakfast of eggs and Spam and then piled into the briefing room. It was a freezing cold point in the morning. Before sunlight could warm us, the inevitable mists so common in England had rolled inland from the North Sea, dripping heavy off buildings and trees and dampening our uniforms the moment we walked outside. We layered ourselves in tiers of clothing to ensure our survival in the sub-zero temperatures that existed four miles above the Earth's surface. Knowing that I couldn't work in the top turret and stay plugged into the bunny suit, I grabbed any available clothing I could wear.

The exhausted grounds crew were readying the Fortresses for the day ahead. They struggled in the bitter cold to load the bombs, finish any last-minute patchwork and stow the ammunition. There was no time to rest or warm themselves. One by one, the crew chief prepared each plane by winding up one of the engines to full power to test its readiness. The surges in sound elevated like the crescendo of a powerful orchestra playing in the darkness until each of the crews was loaded onto the planes. The war was about to begin again. This was mission number 48 for the 96th Bomb Group.

More than 400 of us took a seat in the briefing room, while nervous, anxious chatter questioned what was posted behind the sheet on the wall. It was so dark in many ways. The room hushed as everyone leaned forward to watch the end of the red yarn yank the sheet, announcing the big reveal.

"It's Schweinfurt," the major said with a sarcastic smile. Several in the room muttered their thoughts about this being their last mission. We arrived as a well-trained group of crazy boisterous, young Americans - remember most of us were just 20 to 22 years old. We thought our 27-year-old navigator was an old man and now we were faced with the deepest of realities. Some privately wondered if this was their last day alive.

Attacking the ball bearing factories and marshaling yards in Schweinfurt -- deep in German territory -- a second time was the single most important mission of the Eighth Air Force to date.

The ball bearing was an integral part of the German war industry. Not only did the Germans use a large amount of ball bearings in every aircraft, but ground equipment, such as tanks, cars, trucks and spotlights, did too. Our mission was to destroy the production capability of the enemy. Different estimates had the factories in Schweinfurt producing between forty to fifty five percent of Germany's total output of ball bearings.

Before my crew arrived in England, the Eighth Air Force sustained heavy damage in a complex mission to factories in Schweinfurt and Regensburg on August 17. The First and Third Air Divisions - about sixteen different bomb groups - took to the skies in a dual effort to bomb the production factories of both cities. Timing was critical, as the Third was supposed to penetrate enemy territory ten minutes ahead of the First, in order to divide the Luftwaffe and lesson the amount of fighter opposition each faced. There are about 110 air miles between the two cities. As was frequently the case in the English countryside, Mother Nature did not cooperate. The Third was ordered to take off immediately and the First was grounded in dense fog for nearly three hours. The delay was costly. With three hours between formations the German fighters had time to attack the Third Air

Division, refuel and then take off again to attack the First. Although both targets were significantly damaged, neither was destroyed.

Schweinfurt was a big one. We knew about the first raid, but our crew didn't know a lot about it. Still, we were trying to hit the Germans at their prime.

Sitting in the briefing room that morning we didn't realize how big this mission was going to be. The pre-mission briefing contained everything I needed to know: en route weather, flak concentrations, expected enemy aircraft opposition and so forth. All over England, more than 3,000 airmen left their respective briefing rooms and wondered if the fog would lift so that they could take off or if they would receive the call canceling the mission due to weather. Some 41 planes launched from Snetterton Heath that morning. Just 32 of them were effective on the mission, meaning they made it to the bomb drop.

> The plan consisted of sending 378 aircraft from nineteen bomb groups, which were formed into the three air divisions, over Schweinfurt, according to a report published in the Air and Space Power Journal in 2004 by U.S. Air Force Capt. David Reichert. The First Air Division consisted of nine B-17 bomb groups. The Second Air Division consisted of three B-24 bomb groups. The Third Air Division - my regiment - consisted of seven B-17 bomb groups. (My unit, the 96th Bomb Group, was joined by crews from the 94th, 95th, 100th, 385th, 388th and 390th bomb groups.)
>
> Each division consisted of multiple combat wings, which were organized into combat boxes, the formal term for the tight twenty-one-plane formations. The lead group of the combat wing was placed in the center of the formation, both vertically and horizontally. The second was situated high and behind to the left. To the right and lower was the third group. Less than 1,000 feet separated the highest group from the lowest aircraft in the low group. When a bomber was shot down or had to abort, the remaining bombers would move forward to fill holes in the formation.
>
> The First Air Division was to lead the trail of bombers towards the target, followed by the Third Air Division, which was scheduled to be thirty minutes behind the First and on a parallel course some ten miles south. The Second Air Division was to fly further south of the B-17s and then rendezvous with the other two divisions just prior

to the bomb run, providing a continuous stream of bombers over the target. Almost immediately after take off, the plan fell apart, due to the English weather.

As the bombers began to climb away from their fields, they realized that the weather briefers had been incorrect with their predictions. Instead of breaking out of the low clouds at 2,000 feet, as briefed, most bombers didn't break out until 6,000 feet with some remaining in the clouds until 10,000 feet. Since the bombers needed clear conditions to form up into the combat boxes that afforded them the maximum defensive firepower, the excessive cloud cover over England delayed and in some cases prohibited the bombers from joining with their pre-briefed formations.

The most significant casualty of the weather was the loss of the entire Second Air Division from the combat force. At the pre-briefed rendezvous time, only twenty nine of the sixty B-24s were in formation. After repeated attempts to contact the missing bombers, the air commander of the Second decided against flying into Germany with such an undersized force and instead flew a diversionary mission against the port city of Emden. Without a single bullet being fired, the weather erased sixty bombers and 600 guns from the mission.

We knew if we went into Germany we were going to run into a tremendous volume of antiaircraft artillery. The Germans were well prepared for their factories. They were deeply embedded with dozens of antiaircraft bunkers around their production factories and along the air routes. We also knew we were going to have a tough time with fighter planes. That was a big one.

Yet, we weren't afraid of anything at the time. We never considered being shot down. It just came.

Schweinfurt was an exception to the targets. That was a big target, maybe a two-mile square area where we were eyeballing ten different factory complexes that were multiple streets in length. The 378 planes slated to bomb the city carried a greater payload than any previous mission we saw against key targets with ports and marshaling yards. They were vital, because of the ball bearings. Everything needed ball bearings.

We knew that our crew was it. Once we reached departure altitude and were in formation no one else could do our job, but us. No one could save our lives in the plane, but us. We were never short handed when we flew. If we didn't have enough planes in our own group, we then flew with the 98th, the 100th group and a 300 group. We did that quite often, because the 96th often didn't have enough crews to send formations out on its own. On the Schweinfurt raid, however, everyone flew.

Crew K90 was assigned to fly the Dottie J. III, serial number 42-3348, built by McDonnell Douglas. The previous crew had just finished its 25th mission and was sent home. A gallery of photos donated to the Mighty Eighth Air Force Museum by pilot Moe Woolf's family shows the crew took down twenty four enemy fighters, according to markings on the plane. Military folklore had it that if you completed eight missions your chances of completing twenty five alive were pretty high. We hoped the crew left some good luck for us inside the plane. It's possible we had flown that plane previously, but I wasn't paying attention to the plane's name.

The earth seemed to tremble as we took off from the main runway at Snetterton Heath and headed east, as the English countryside faded from view. At 19,000 feet the English Channel looked small enough to long jump over. We climbed over the marshes and double estuary in the peninsula known as the Naze about midday and left the beach at Clacton-on-Sea. Across the English Channel, we traveled in a straight line toward Germany, traversing the southwestern corner of the Netherlands and just south of Antwerp in Belgium. Once we reached the German border at Aachen we headed south to the Mosel River.

While our Third Air Division approached the target relatively unscathed the First Air Division was already under attack at Aachen. We began to hear chatter on the radios from units ahead of us.

Charging ahead at 22,000 feet, we banked west at Luxembourg. The visibility was eight to twelve miles along the course. The Initial Point or IP was at the Main River north of Wurzburg when we spaced ourselves behind the leading wing. This was sweating time. We flew straight and level with the bomb bay doors open. Normally, the IP happened about twenty miles from the target. Descending to the bombardier-controlling height of 20,000 feet Bill Kieran began giving the pilots instructions on maintaining altitude and air speed as we approached Schweinfurt from the West.

All the while, I was anxiously watching the skies, always looking for something.

We arrived on target about ten minutes after the First Air Division at 2:50 p.m. We could see flak in the distance. Gas and oil fires were dotting the countryside, evidence of the merciless defense made by the First. The entire city was blanketed in blackish grey smoke. It was thicker and more dense than the white foggy clouds we pulled out of England on.

Some crews in the Third couldn't set up and follow the PDI (pilot direction instrument). Having no other options the lead bombardier set his crosshairs on a bridge to the southwest of the factories. On his mark the entire division of Forts dropped their bombs, primarily on the southern half of the factory complexes and the marshaling yards that led from the city to Wurzburg. There were isolated patches of clearance, however, that allowed some planes to break through and drop ten bombs at the MPI (maximum point of impact). Those individual stories have been recorded in the personal histories of other survivors. We didn't have any problems getting in there or Bill Kieran would have said something.

We felt the first WHUMPS of flak over the target, but still managed to drop ten notes to Adolf Hitler on explosive 500-pound envelopes and pull away. Oh, we hit our targets! With our mission complete we turned to follow the First back to the fighter escorts, hoping for some beleaguered relief from the Luftwaffe as our fuel supply diminished. That's when our fire fight began, however.

Suddenly out of nowhere, the Luftwaffe began ferociously attacking us. We were met with single engine Focke-Wulf 190s and Messerschmitt 109s that came directly at our formations, firing 20-millimeter cannons and machine guns. From behind twin-engine Messerschmitt 110s and 210s tailed beyond our range and shot crude rockets into our formations.

We had been briefed to anticipate 500 or so enemy fighters along the route. There were more, maybe 700. We didn't expect all that came at us. Dozens of earthen bunkers with multiple antiaircraft guns guarded the city from both the north and south across the river. One of the goals of the flak barrages, in addition to damaging and shooting down planes, was to disrupt the bomber formations and ruin their aim.

There was a wall of flak in front of us. When the Germans unleashed their cannons it was like thousands of flashbulbs and spotlights going off consecutively. When those things burst in the sky it would be completely black in front of us. The only way we could avoid a complete invasion was to swerve to avoid it. Lt. Bye would turn toward the one that just exploded, knowing the Germans needed a few minutes to reload the antiaircraft guns. There was no place you could really go. I fought to control my guns and relied on my tracers.

Sometimes we didn't miss the flak, but it didn't cause much damage to our plane. I could hear the bullets entering through one side of the plane and rattling the rig's interior as they exited the other side.

We battled fighters for more than an hour as we raced toward France. Time seemed to stand still in the turret, even while I was frantically calling off fighter locations. I battled those I could see, but I couldn't help notice the ranks of bombers were thinning around us. Our precise formations were becoming ragged.

Suddenly a plane next in formation would be struck by one of the devastating rockets and pieces of the plane and crewmen made their miles-long descent to earth. The crews of planes with titles such as Windy City Avenger, Hard Luck, Carolina Boomerang, The Big Moose, Thunderbolt, Old Faithful and The Natural gave their all that day.

Luckily, my machine gun triggers never jammed. I always took good care of my guns. We were supposed to shoot them in short bursts. Otherwise the barrels would burn out. At this moment, however, planes were coming at us three and four at a time. We would battle one group for a few minutes and then they'd turn away, just as another group of three or four barreled down on us from another direction. I aimed everything on the Messerschmitts coming up behind us. As the formations thinned out we were left short, which allowed fighter planes to get closer to us. I could see our tracers going through their planes. We dropped our entire payload that day and, I'm sure, we all burned out our machine gun barrels on our way to the ground.

At some point we couldn't keep up with the formation. The dreaded slow down had begun about ten miles away from the target on our return. Every pilot fears a slow down at the front of the formation might cause the other planes to overrun the group. We, on the other hand, were lagging behind.

It was about 4 o'clock in the afternoon. We were flying just outside of Thiaucourt, France. The autumn sun was making its graceful orange bow into the night and we still had cannons being fired at us from every direction. One got close enough for Lt. Bye to look into the eyes of the opposing pilot. That may have been Lt. Eberhard Schade, the German fighter credited with taking us down. The right wing of our plane was on fire. The control cables were shot out. The oxygen and interphone weren't working. All the engines were gone. One was hit by antiaircraft.

Lt. Bye always said if we couldn't maintain formation he would head toward the tree tops and we'd go to Switzerland where we would be interned.

We took a hard steep dive. The plane was going down. Yet, we still had a group of enemy fighters following us all the way down and shooting. The Germans believed that if they had a crippled plane it was better to ensure it was shot down than to waste critical moments shooting on others. Spiraling down, we still shot back. Oh, I know we got a couple of them. I saw two giant plumes of black smoke rising off in the distance. I knew we shot down two planes, even though I never could verify it.

Each of us had a parachute that strapped to the front of our flight suits, in case we had to bail out. I couldn't move in the turret with the chute on. So I often placed it on the floor behind the pilots' seats. As we began to brace ourselves to crash I looked down from the top turret for my chute, only to realize it skidded forward into the nose. If we had to bail out I would have been a goner.

Lt. Bye informed us we were going to land and he told everyone to get into a safe position on the floor in the radio room. I raced down the post, crouching on the floor behind Lt. Bye's seat, my feet braced against the base of the turret and my head in my gloves. All I could feel was the frightful way my heart thundered. There was no safety equipment to prevent us from being tossed around or thrown from the aircraft. It only took a few minutes. We passed a farm house and crossed over the top of freshly plowed fields where a small group of people were just finishing up their day's work. We belly flopped that plane into a long burning wedge across one of those fields. Our landing gear was still up. The plane was decimated. The only portion that remained was the tail section and a bit of the belly.

We all survived, because Lt. Bye did a darn good job landing that plane.

The rising heat and choking smell of burning aviation fuel began to overwhelm us. We had to escape quickly. Our escape kits were in our pockets filled with foreign money, maps, a compass, clear water and some penicillin. Lt. Bye had forgotten to destroy the Norden Bombsight and reentered the plane to shoot his revolver into a hole at the top. We didn't want the Germans to get ahold of it. We had no other artillery, just our machine guns.

When we got out, I didn't know the tail gunner Alton Baer, Jr got shot in the leg or that both waist gunners Michael Olynik and Charles Gattman were shot on the side and head, respectively. They were wearing antiaircraft flak suits, which were aprons with metal on the front and the back. The sides were open, however. Frederick Holt, the ball turret gunner, and I took Charles Gattman with us. We patched him up as best we could.

In the distance I could see local farmers already digging holes to bury our parachutes. They were constructed of sturdy nylon fabric, which was scarce those days. No locals ever came up to me, but Lt. Bye's daughter Brigid O'Donnell told me that a farmer approached her father, asking for ammunition and the right to pilfer the plane for his cabinet business.

I took one last look at our handiwork, as the two black smoke clouds of burning enemy fighters continued to repaint the western sky.

We had to split up. There was no discussion as a group about where to go or what to do. We weren't even certain what country we were in. At that moment our military tour together splintered into ten different directions with ten different story lines. We didn't want to get captured there. We simply ran like hell to get away from the plane. We ran for miles until we got to the woods. There we stayed overnight.

The United States Army Air Forces lost sixty planes and 600 men that October afternoon. It was the single deadliest mission in World War II. Forever, it will be known as Black Thursday.

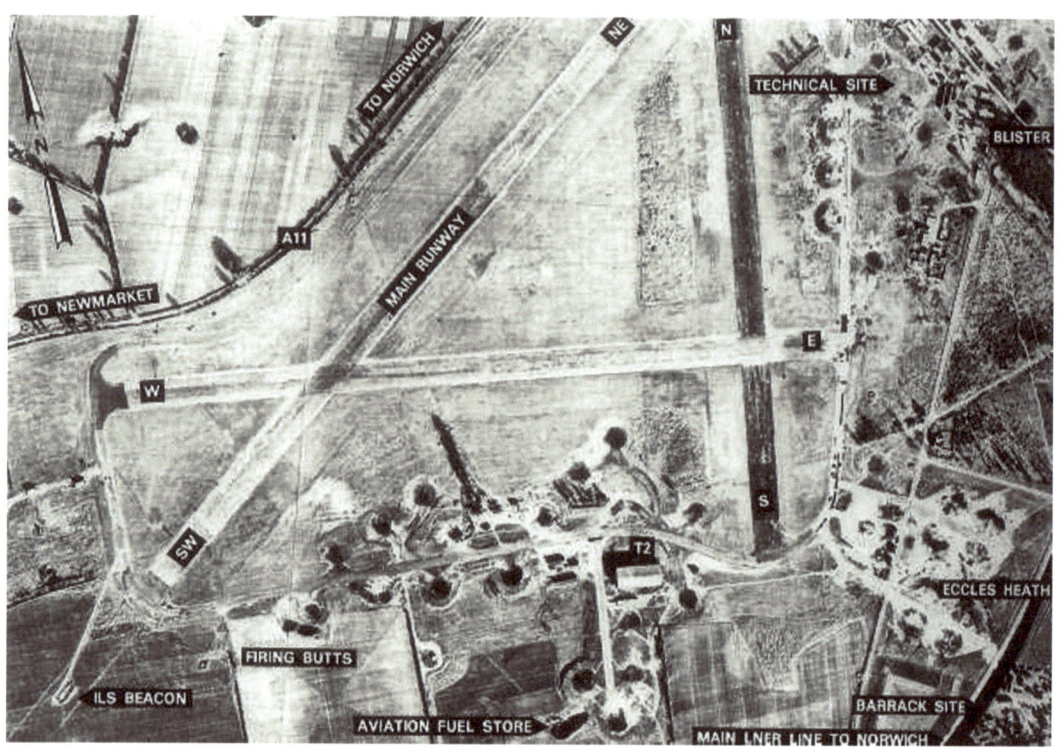

(Above) Snetterton Heath Air Force base, UK. (Left) The Dottie J III B-17 bomber after it crashed in a farm field outside Thiaucourt, France, showing plane from left side. German officer and tent under the wing. Photo here and opposite page provided from the private collection of Brigid Bye O'Donnell and reproduced with permission.

(Above) The Dottie J III B-17 bomber after it crashed in a farm field outside Thiaucourt, France, showing plane from right side. German officer standing in the back behind burned out engine. (Right) Ariel photo of Stalag XVIIB (right) outside Krems, Austria.

This Certificate of Merit was earned by Gerard Caporaso for completing a 13-week course in algebra at the Interned Airmen's Institute at Stalag XVIIB, dated Feb. 9, 1945. It was signed by the camper leader Kenneth J. Kurtenbach and educational director Alexander M. Haddrow.

Gerard Caporaso's final letter home after the war ended, dated May 17, 1945.

Gerard J. Caporaso standing outside the barracks after receiving his Honorable Discharge from military service in Syracuse, New York on Nov. 16, 1945.

Chapter 8

CAPTURED

Hidden under the darkness of France's eastern woodlands, we were acutely aware that any noise we made could give us away to the enemy. The subtle rustling of our flight suits. Our steaming breath against the freezing night sky or the growling eruption that signaled our empty guts like a dinner bell.

We couldn't stay hidden. Under the light of the full moon hovering over France, Fred, Charles and I stretched out our maps to figure out our orientation. We didn't know where we were or even what country we were in. From where we were stranded we needed to head west to get back to England.

We started marching across plowed farmlands and fields.

We were ravenous. There was no food in the escape packs, just a dark chocolate bar, and our crew typically didn't carry any food or coffee with us on missions. We didn't know what we were going to eat now. At one point we crossed a freshly plowed field and realized there was some stray produce on the ground. We thought they may have been rutabagas. They were a good size round, larger than an orange and smaller than a cantaloupe. We stockpiled two each in our pockets and kept moving.

Every so often we'd see a car driving down the road all blackened out with little slits left open on the headlights so the driver could see. Unsure whether there were Gestapo agents in those cars or locals going about their business, we dove into ditches and hid our faces and hands. Certainly, the full moon could give us away.

We walked all night long. The weather was fine, but cool. Along the road we saw a street sign with the name of a town nearby and knew we were in France. The night sky in the country is blacker than black. No street lights lined our route. No distant city lighted the atmosphere. Were it not for the full moon we would have had a tougher time trying to escape. As the midnight hours began to dawn we decided to head for cover among the trees again.

We approached the edge of the woods just as three soldiers walked out and aimed their machine guns at us. We were surrounded. At first, we didn't know if they were French or German. Remember, we recognized airplanes. Ground troops were different. I asked them if they were French and they shook their heads no. Somehow in all the yelling we understood they were German. One of us reached into our pockets to offer up one of the rutabagas as a peace offering and the guards instantly jumped their guns on us. They thought we were pulling a grenade on them.

They took us all the way back to a village just south of where we crash landed. Before we knew it the room was filled with big shot German brass. The interrogation was rigid as they tried to prod, bribe and threaten information out of us. We couldn't tell them anything, except our name, rank and serial number. They knew it, too, but they were hoping to get something out of us. After an hour or so a senior ranking officer came in, who must have been a general. He had big red lapels and all these metals on his jacket. Everyone saluted him. He, too, tried to get more information out of us, but he couldn't.

"Name one of your crew members and we'll let you go," he repeated.

I didn't. I gave him a false name and the others did, too. Eventually, he got frustrated and let us go so we could be sent to the prison camp.

The Gestapo agents were amazed with our escape kits. They were generally a brown paper envelope bearing a large red "F" for France. Inside was a cloth map of France showing escape routes to Switzerland, a small steel hacksaw blade in a cardboard container, French money, a hard chocolate bar sometimes and a tiny compass the size of a dime that could be hidden on a person.

The small compasses fascinated them with their itsy-bitsy rotating hands signaling north, south, east and west. They were amazed. They took all that stuff away from us.

After our interrogation we were told to empty our pockets. Thank goodness we learned not to bring anything personal with us, such as address books, photos or, even, a matchbook. Officials didn't want the Gestapo to know where we were located in England. The only thing we were carrying were our escape kits and those ripe rutabagas.

The next few days were the start of 24 months that I spent years trying to forget. My youth, my life, was on hold at the hands of the Gestapo. Nothing in our training really prepared us to be captured. There was some discussion about being a prisoner of war, but it was a white wash over reality. We were treated roughly.

From there we spent a few days in solitary confinement. It was the first step in stripping us of our dignity. That was the scariest part of it. The cell was a concrete tomb seven or eight feet wide by ten feet long. A tiny little window at the top was all that provided us with sunshine. Through a small door at the bottom they'd push a minuscule amount of food rations each day.

That was it. We'd be stuck between the walls all day long. Sitting. Standing. Stooped over. Every once in a while, they would take us out during the day for a half hour to get some air. They'd take us in for interrogation where they repeatedly quizzed us on our base whereabouts, missions, crew members and more. Again, we told them nothing: same old name, rank and serial number.

One day I heard a radio show where Axis Sally, a German-American radio personality named Mildred Gillars, broadcast propaganda for Nazi Germany radio. She reported the details of our plane being shot down and listed all the crew members. It's tough to hear bad news of yourself on a broadcast.

A few days later we were put into the back seat of three separate cars with German guards on either side of us and one in the front seat. Leading the pack was a German guard in a separate vehicle. They thought they had a parade, a public spectacle of what they called Luft Gangsters all the way to the train station that would ferry us to the prison camp. We weren't the only ones taken to the station. While standing on the wooden platform waiting for the trains to arrive, a group of Hitler youths in uniforms carrying knives approached us. They tried to lunge at us with their knives drawn when the guards chased them back with their guns. We had nothing to fight them with and we were surrounded by German guards. Because we didn't speak the language, we didn't understand what they were saying. The derision and cockiness of their body language spoke volumes, however. Surprisingly enough, the German guards protected us. We easily could have been killed.

That scared us, because they really wanted to kill us and they were all trained. Until that point we were still holding on to our own youthful bravery. We weren't afraid of anything until those kids threatened us.

From the rail station we were forced to stand for several hours on the train to Frankfurt, Germany where we were interrogated and again jailed in solitary confinement for a week or two. That, too, was extremely frightening, because I didn't have anyone to talk to.

When the decision came to take us to the prison camp several hundred prisoners were corralled to a marshaling yard where they pushed us into freight cars, boxed up like goods with no room to breathe, let alone move. We didn't even have the room to lay down. At best, we could squat.

We lingered for hours in a long string of box cars where the only thing we were sure of was our own ragged existence. We were tired, hungry, dirty, and scared. Every emotion, every sound and all our fears elevated jointly. The nauseating smell of combined dried sweat wafted in the air, burning our eyes. Our breath heated the cars. Whatever happened to us happened together. Suddenly, we heard the familiar roar of an approaching air raid off in the distance. We understood all those familiar sounds and aviation movements from the air. Frankfurt's marshaling yards were frequent targets of the strategic bombing program. The German guards left the trains, locked the doors so we couldn't escape, and abandoned us for the safety of their own air raid shelters.

We were sitting ducks in cheap metal caskets while the Royal Air Force bombed the heck out of the marshaling yards. A giant bullseye. The bombs exploded all around us and we could feel the ground erupting below our feet. Some bombs hit the neighborhood next door. For a long terrifying moment - maybe half an hour - we waited to die, and prayed we didn't. Luckily those prayers were answered and the English didn't hit us. We were very fortunate.

A few hours later the guards returned and the engines jerked forward, throwing us sideways and backward against the walls of the freight car. We were shuttled through Berlin to Krems, Austria. There groups of postulating guards shaking rifle butts at us bum rushed us off the train and marched us up a long hill.

Stalag XVIIB looked like a large farm, except it was surrounded by two layers of barbed wire, guard towers on each corner and a dozen angry German shepherds.

Letter Home - Stalag XVIIB
Sunday, Nov. 28, 1943
Dear Mom,
I hope you know by now that I'm safe and feeling fine. How is everyone at home? How is Betty? She must be getting big now. Tell her I'll be home as soon as the war is over. It should not be long now. We don't have much to do here. We have some books to read, cards and checkers, but outside of that there's not much to do. I have been a prisoner of war for six weeks now. I hope you spent a better Thanksgiving than we did. I'll make up for it when I get home. If this letter reaches you by Christmas, keep one of my allotments and buy Christmas presents for

everyone. Buy Betty anything she wants. I'll have a lot of pay coming by the time I get out of here. Send me some cigarettes and write as soon and often as you can. Give my regards to everyone. Merry Christmas and Happy New Year.
Love, Jerry

Chapter 9

SURVIVING STALAG XVII B

If there was ever a possibility to witness a slow decent to hell while still alive here on earth then it could be seen inside the double barbed-wire walls lining Stalag XVII B in the village of Gneixendorf, just outside Krems, Austria.

Imprisoned for 19 months, I watched brutal German guards taking hostile command of their perceived authority on life, slowly peeling away every layer of a man's dignity. Our freedom of movement went first. As the camp's population doubled in size to nearly 30,000 prisoners of war, including 4,200 Americans, we were stripped of our humanity, masculinity, and mental health. It was the slow and deplorable way they chipped away at our physical health by feeding us rotten maggot-infested food or no food at all that starved us of any physical strength we had to fight for our lives.

The Germans did everything possible, just short of a complete violation of the Third Geneva Convention of 1929, to starve us to death. The Russian prisoners of war were not so lucky. The Germans didn't give them anything, not a blessed thing.

They could not, however, touch our faith in God, the American spirit, creativity that's fueled by a camp full of engineers with idle time, or the soldier's bond. While at the end of our stay in Stalag XVII B many of us were walking shells of a human being, it was my faith and my belief in our country that helped to keep me alive.

I was Luft gangster number 99959, housed in Barracks 37.

From Berlin, our freight train arrived in Krems, where the city's main train station is a junction of four major railways. We were shuttled under heavy guard a few miles north to Gneixendorf and marched by twos up a long hill to the prison camp. It looked like a big farm, except there was a tower on every corner and gnarly guards patrolled halfway down each side with trained German Shepherds. We were well guarded. There was no question about it.

Fred Holt and I were still together. We were among the earliest groups to arrive. Once we got settled into our barracks at the camp we met other guys that we flew with, not from our crew, but from our base.

Nestled in a farming community, Stalag XVII B was situated about 100 meters northwest of the village of Gneixendorf, between Krems and Langenlois. It was previously used as a concentration camp when prisoners of war from France, Italy and Russia began to arrive. On October 13, 1943, just a day before the second raid on Schweinfurt occurred, some 1,350 noncommissioned Air Force personnel from Stalag VIIA were transferred to Stalag XVII B. There was a steady stream of non commissioned officers funneling into the camp daily until the U.S. ranks reached 4,237 prisoners.

The American prisoners occupied five compounds that were approximately 175 yards long by 75 yards wide. They contained four double barracks that were 100 by 240 feet long and built to accommodate 240 men. At least 4,000 U.S. prisoners crammed into space designed for maybe 1,800 men. During the day we could walk between the compounds. If, however, the Germans wanted to shut off a particular compound they would lock the gate. Over time, as other arrivals made their way into the camp, we began to recognize soldiers from training or Snetterton Heath.

In the center of each barracks was a washroom with six basins. There was no hot water and the Germans often gave us no access to water at all during the day.

They turned it on for a few minutes in the morning, often before 6:30 a.m., and at mealtime. We had to gather it quickly to wash our ourselves and our Air Force clothing and have water to drink and cook. As such, we were always collecting spare cans to save water in. The sleeping quarters had triple deck bunk beds stacked in rows. We would use the bottom bunk for storage and then guys would double up in the beds to stay warm. The mattresses were canvas sacks filled with straw, which we had to take outside and fluff up every few days. Bugs and lice were a big problem in the camp.

The Germans made certain we were absolutely miserable. Each barracks had just one coal stove that we used to cook and stay warm. One stove for several hundred men. The fuel ration was one 50-pound bucket of coal per week, which was only enough fuel for a day. It didn't go far. We were constantly conserving and trying to find ways to stay warm in the blustery Austrian winters. That in itself caused the prisoners to take desperate measures. Over time bits and pieces of the buildings started to disappear.

The guards would conduct their rounds at night and then move on to other details. By the morning light, soldiers had quietly begun to strip away at the outside of all the buildings, tearing wood off that could be burned for fuel. First the front and rear porches on either end of the barracks disappeared. Fence posts went missing. Finally, they began to tear off the sides of buildings, leaving gaping holes and leaking roofs. Shingles, railings, floor boards, and other garbage were all burned. The Germans couldn't do anything about it, because they didn't know when it was being done and we weren't making noise about it. We had lookouts. We'd sneak around either between or after their rounds.

Everybody wasn't in on everything. We had certain guys who would rip down the boards and others who would tunnel. The system worked out pretty well.

The prison camp was situated in the middle of a large farming community. There was no way to escape. The only way to get out was to tunnel. Well, we had all kind of tunnels. A group of American prisoners attempted to build one very long tunnel across our barracks and into the neighboring compound. Between guards patrols or late at night they would move the coal stove and dig underneath it, pushing piles of dirt back up into the barracks like an assembly line. Everyone would come to visit that barracks. All the fellows put dirt into their pockets and wandered around the courtyard the next day, slowly dropping bits and pieces. We must have looked like a dust cloud.

They got fairly close to completing it when the Germans discovered the tunnel near the end of the War. Whenever we got too far they could find things. I don't know how they did it. Sometimes I think the dogs could figure out that there were people underneath the ground and signaled their handlers that somebody was down there.

Even if they did manage to tunnel through to freedom, not many people could have gone. I wouldn't go. We were way over in eastern Austria. We needed to be able to speak the language. I didn't. Where was I going to go? I didn't know the land or even where I was. To survive an escape attempt we needed to be able to do things like cross rivers. If we couldn't swim, we would be in trouble. We needed a boat to get across the Danube River, along the Krems border. I didn't know how to steal a boat, either.

Several times over the course of the 19 months in the prison camp, we received donated civilian clothing from the guards and coats from the International Red Cross. If we were able to tunnel out I supposed we could have put on civilian clothing and gone undetected for a while. Still, I needed to know the language. It was no good. We were in a bad position. That was a bad camp. The Germans hated to have anyone escape from a prison camp.

One soldier did escape, I think, during a work detail outside of the prison camp. After a couple of days they caught him and brought him back. He spent 30 days in solitary confinement. Solitary was a little wooden shack, no lights. No nothing. That was tough.

On another occasion two soldiers attempted to escape and it nearly took down the camp. Some of their friends and people in the camp might have known they were trying to escape, but I didn't know. One escaped. The other man tried to go through the barbed wire and was shot by the guards.

Between the camps were two rows of barbed wire. The Germans used to collect our used cans and bottles from the Red Cross parcels that were occasionally sent to us and threw them between the barbed wire. If anyone tried to cross the wire either the garbage made a huge racket or the soldier got cut up in the process.

Along the fence was a lame little sign warning us that any prisoners attempting to cross the barbed wire boundary would be instantly shot. They weren't kidding.

During that escape attempt the Germans decided to unleash their pent-up anger and ran roughshod like psychotic cowboys, shooting their guns in every direction, especially into the open doorways of the barracks. These were a few dozen angry prison guards, who were assigned to camp duty rather than the front lines or the Luftwaffe. They were angry at their own lot in life and had no problem taking down weakened soldiers with their rifle butts if they didn't move fast enough. I hit the deck when bullets came flying through my barracks. None came near me, thankfully. Under the guise of shooting at escaping POWs, the guards tried to clean house by taking down a few other prisoners. They scared the lights out of us. We had a rough time there for a while.

In the end, they shot both men. The one who escaped was eventually caught and thrown into solitary confinement for 370 days. He never did get out of that little room. That's rough.

To throw the Germans off guard we built plenty of dummy tunnels. We build fake ones that were easier to find. That worked for a long, long time. But eventually they found everything.

The only thing we were authorized – commanded, really – to dig was an air raid shelter for ourselves. These big trenches were four to five feet deep and about three feet wide. They snaked around the camp. In Austria's constantly wet weather these shelters frequently became a moat. Every so often we'd have an air raid warning while the ground was wet and someone would dive head first into a mud bath. We even had a dummy tunnel in there, too. They found it, but we didn't care.

> Letter home - Dec. 12, 1943
> German ID: 99959
> *Dear Mom*
> *I am writing again. I'm safe and well here. There's not much to write about. I am only waiting for the war to end. We have quite a bit of snow here. It's about what we have at home. Austria is a pretty clean country, what I saw of it. But I'll be glad to get out of here and come home. How is everyone? Give Betty a kiss for me and tell her to be good. Wish Lucy a Happy Birthday for me. I think today is her birthday. I hope you get in touch with the Red Cross and send me a*

parcel. Send me cigarettes and chocolate bars or anything to eat. It's getting close to Christmas. So I wish you all a Merry Christmas. Say hello to all my friends for me and please write soon.
Love Jerry

Food. We lived without it and we lived for it. We dreamed about food, talked about food and cheered any day that food arrived. We held lengthy conversations, describing in elaborate details all the food we planned to eat when we returned home and how it was all prepared.

Soup was the only thing on the menu in prison camp. The Germans gave us giant metal buckets of soup each day, often filled with rotten food and maggots. Man, they tasted good, too. When you have nothing to eat everything tastes really good. Occasionally, the Germans gave us small loaves of dense black bread the size of a man's fist. It was enough for one slice for four men. That's all we ate the entire day.

Sometimes my barracks got a half of a loaf of long bread. Sometimes we got a little more and sometimes we got a little less. The fellow slicing the bread served himself last. We devoured it quickly.

Twice I remember them bringing in potatoes. They were all rotten. They must have been the end of the heap. We had to share them among all the people in my barracks. My buddy and I got one little potato. We sliced it up and fried it on top of the stove.

We were supposed to get a Red Cross parcel every month that was supplied by the U.S. Army.

The standard American Red Cross Package we received weighed about nine pounds and contained a small can of Spam, a small container of jelly, instant coffee, a Disney chocolate bar, an eight ounce piece of cheese, hardtack biscuits, a can of powdered milk, a can of oleomargarine and cigarettes. My sons tease me about eating Spam, but I liked it. Man, did we make that last.

Sometimes the Germans wouldn't give the packages to us. They had every excuse in the world. Sometimes they'd say they weren't shipped or the deliveries got bombed out. They were notorious for poking holes in the cans with their bayonets. Often we had to share a package with three or four people. I don't ever remember having a package to myself. I always shared mine with a buddy named Lindsey from Massachusetts. We shared a bunk together.

All the while I wrote home telling my mother that I received a package every Friday and had plenty to eat.

We were supposed to get shaving equipment, too. Half the time we didn't even shave, because the equipment never arrived. The International Red Cross began conducting periodic wellness checks of the camp in January 1944. Before they arrived the Germans always gave us another wool blanket for our bunks to show they were really taking care of us. The following day they took them all away.

The Red Cross packages filled two needs. There wasn't anything fed to us by the Germans that was remotely nutritious, let alone satisfying in its abundance. These boxes represented grand feasts that we could only fantasize about for months. In my eyes that little can of Spam was like a slowly roasted Thanksgiving turkey dripping in butter and sage. The cheese would do until I could taste my mother's Italian cooking again. We longed for a good cup of brew: coffee with milk. As weak as I was, these parcels kept me standing.

They also fulfilled our weary inner need for any connection to the outside world. Any mental stimulation at all. They were made in America, filled with cans of food typically eaten in the United States and had labels in English. They refilled our belief that the United States government wouldn't let us down. They knew we were there. That in itself gave us hope.

The arrival of Red Cross parcels was known as Pay Day. No matter when they arrived at camp, Pay Day was always on Friday. We savored and hoarded every bit. Quite a few prisoners smoked. I smoked. When we got a pack, we'd light one up, take one puff and then put it out. Later on in the day, if we wanted another cigarette, we'd take another puff. We had to make them last. We had to. We all had these instant coffee cans. When we got down to the end of the cigarette we'd put it out in the can and then open up the entire paper. Eventually we had enough butts to smoke another cigarette. We'd smoke all the nicotine straight through.

Because everything was scarce, the contents of those parcels were negotiable like money. Cigarettes and chocolate, which we called D bars, were extremely valuable. We used to play poker and bridge in camp. Those who didn't smoke used the cigarettes for money. Every aspect of the box and its contents was reused. Even the giant shipping crates they came in were burned for firewood.

Letter Home - March 24, 1944
Gefangenennummer: 99959

Dear Mom,
Every letter I write from here becomes harder because there isn't much to write about. I'm feeling good so please don't worry about me. I hope everyone at home is feeling fine. How's Betty? I guess I won't know her when I see her again. She'll be old enough to go to school pretty soon. Well we got our Red Cross parcels today. I don't think I told you that we get a parcel from the Red Cross every week, besides the food that the Germans feed us. We also get quite a few clothes from the Red Cross. They take care of us pretty well. I wish you would write as soon as you can. See the Red Cross about sending mail. It's pretty windy here, but it snows almost every day. We're used to it now. Well Mom, I'll close now, because we have to get up at 6:30 in the morning to shower. Give my regards to everyone.
Love your son,
Jerry

You can't have a camp full of Army Air Force engineers with idle time and trash and not expect something ingenious to happen. We saved the cans from our parcels and found endless ways to recycle them. Guys would make handles for the cans so we could make cups. Using stones like cave men, they flattened large cans for plates and retooled smaller cans for bowls. The can we used the most was the one-pound oleomargarine can. We'd make a big strap for a handle to go around it. Our former Spam containers became our drinking glasses, shaving cups, barracks gutters, soup bowls, scoops and anything else we imagined. Somewhere in the camp several guys rigged up a still and passed around the moonshine at the next holiday, much to our delight. It was really great when I start to think of all the things that were created there.

We even made lamps using our one-pound margarine containers. We made wicks out of a piece of string that we found somewhere or pulled out of a bit of clothing or our mattresses. At night, after the Germans conducted their second round and shut off the lights, we would burn the margarine and play cards by dim candle light. We weren't worried about saving the margarine. What were we going to butter? We didn't have any food.

Everyone had a piece of someone else's handiwork.

Every Air Force crew had two trained radio operators, two engineers, and two armorers. The radio operators were in our camp. Over time they found a way to create vacuum tubes with old instant coffee cans. I don't know how they did it, but they managed to get all the air out of the cans and create a vacuum. Somehow they created radios that were able to pick up broadcasts from the British Broadcasting Corporation (BBC). We had several radios in the camp. After we were there a while someone was assigned to come to our barracks each day and read off news from the BBC. That's how we knew what was going on. We knew how far the United States was advancing and when they were advancing. Coupled with information we received from newer prisoners, we knew we were winning the war. The allied troops were not far away from our camp. We were still there and, as such, we created problems for the Germans. They were commanded to supply us with food and they also had to provide our camp with guards, who could have been fighting on the front lines. Boy, did we start giving the Germans a hard time. We knew we were going home. We just had to stay alive to get there.

We had some genius radio operators with us.

> Letter from Home - Spring 1944
> *Dear Jerry,*
> *We are all feeling fine and hope to hear the same from you too. Well Jerry, another Easter has passed without you here and I'm sure you will be with us before the next Easter. All we can do is to hope and pray that it is to end soon. Keep you chin up and don't worry about anything. Try to be cheerful and keep busy to pass the time. We took pictures yesterday and I'll send some when I get them back. May you be home before you ever get them. We all hope so. Give our regards to Baer, Gattman and Holt. Mom and Dad send their love and Betty sends a big hug and a kiss. All the neighbors send their regards. Take care of yourself. Soon.*
> *Love Lu*
> (My sister Lucy wrote the letter for my mother.)

The one tool we had at our fingertips was our military-issued P-38 can opener, a small hinged piece of metal about one and a half inches long that looked like a

FROM THE TOP TURRET

folded over razor blade. It consisted of a short metal blade that served as a handle and a small, hinged metal hook that folds out to pierce the lid of a can. The P-38 hung with my dog tags on a chain around my neck. Mine was in good shape, because I didn't use it much until I got to camp. It worked very well. A P-38 could also be used as scissors, a screw driver, nail file, scraper, bottle opener, stripper, chisel, coffee stirrer, cooking utensil, or hair clipper, if needed. It could be spent for barter or used to signal Morse code.

After we were in camp for a while we were allowed to write airmail letters home. It took many months to anything to arrive in camp and it took just as long for my parents to receive any information at all about my existence. I am sure the worry weighed heavy on my mother.

In the letters homes, we weren't allowed to mention anything about our whereabouts or the War. Otherwise, the censor would cut it out. We were warned and I made it a practice not to be blacked out by the censor. There was a systematic way about the content of my letters. It felt like I was simply putting my name on a piece of paper. I opened by telling her that I was fine and immediately shifting the conversation to asked about the family, my friends and my baby sister Betty, who was born the day I graduated high school. If you analyzed the letters in a pile you could tell something wasn't right. I went from telling my mother that there wasn't much to do in prison camp to telling her that I started a garden.. I told her there was plenty to eat and we received Red Cross parcels each week, when in fact none of that was true. I told her I was tired a lot and slept often. Individually a censor couldn't see anything was amiss. Collectively, my family could only recognize my handwriting and know that I was still alive.

> Letter home - August 22, 1944
> Gefangenennummer 99959
> *Dear Mom,*
> *I haven't written to you for quite awhile, so I thought I'd write a few lines tonight. I'm feeling fine and everything is getting along okay. How is everyone at home? Fred Holt and Gattman both received letters and parcels from home. Baer did also. I'm glad you wrote to Fred's sister. I hope you wrote to the other families of the rest of the crew too. I have been working lately to help pass the time away.*

I'm helping to fix library books. It's easy and it makes the time pass faster.
How is Betty? Tell her I'm always thinking of her and the rest of you.
I hope to see you all in the near future. That's all for now, so I'll close.
Say hello to all of my friends for me.
Love your son, Jerry

Camp prisoners set up their own form of government. At the top there was an elected Man of Communications or a Man of Command, who would speak on behalf of the prisoners to the German guards. He was an American soldier who spoke German. You couldn't just approach any German guard with your concerns, because if they got caught talking to you they could also be shot.

The Man of Command was like a governor. In each barracks was a chosen leader, like a mayor, who reported to and from the Man of Command. It was through these channels that they tried to negotiate with the Germans for more privileges.

The Germans weren't readily giving us anything extra: certainly no food, clothing or fuel. Those who could trade, traded. A fellow in our camp named Ben Phelper traded cigarettes and chocolate for a camera and several rolls of film from an Italian prisoner. During his time in camp he kept a well-hidden diary, written on the back of Red Cross parcels. After the war, he published a memoir called Kriege Memories with rare photos from inside the prison camp. He was only able to accomplish that feat, because he befriended a German guard who often took photos for him.

As a group, we were able to negotiate permission to build a chapel and practice our faith. The chapel was built in an empty barracks. We took old crates and made benches, with small wooden boxes. A group of fellows made a beautiful paper crucifix out of recycled Red Cross parcels. The Germans gave us paint to white wash the inside of the chapel. A French prisoner said mass for the Catholics on Sunday. He conducted the service as best he could and gave a sermon. It was quite a change. You'd be surprised how many people attended a religious service in a prison camp each week without fail.

We would go out and walk a lot. That was as much as we could do to keep ourselves mentally and physically fit. By the springtime we were restless. A group other than the Red Cross, maybe the Y.M.C.A. or the Salvation Army, eventually sent us all types of sports equipment, including baseballs, basketballs, bocce sets, horse shoes, and even boxing gloves.

A boxing ring was set up on a spare mound of dirt inside one of the compounds. We created baseball diamonds where ever we could. There was a formal, larger diamond set up in the main area, but just outside our barracks we often played pickup games with anyone who wanted to play. If the ball went over the fence it would kill the day until we could persuade a German guard to retrieve it.

By summertime, the Germans knew we had a national holiday coming up on July 4. Camp leaders negotiated for the right to host an Independence Day celebration and the Germans agreed to have only one roll call in the morning. They gave us nothing else. In a show of true old fashioned American spirit we set up a grand celebration complete with baseball games all afternoon, a rousing patriotic sing-a-long, and inspirational speeches from the commanders reminding us that we came, we fought and we were still conquering. The infusion of positive spirit was just what we needed to boost our morale.

The musicians in camp sang a lot. Newer prisoners brought with them entertainment news. They knew all the latest songs and that, somehow, the dance halls across England and the United States were switching from the shag to swing dancing. The song we sang frequently in camp was Mairzy Doats by The Merry Macs. Sometimes the fellows put on small skits. Toward the end of the War, the Germans started showing us some of their popular films.

One privilege I got to participate in was honoring fallen soldiers at their burial. The camp cemetery was tucked under a group of trees a short distance from the eastern edge of camp, just outside the barbed wire fence. American soldiers were laid to rest in simple wooden boxes the Germans made. We'd line up and salute the coffins as they passed by the fence. I got to know many people in camp, their names and hometowns slowly slipping from my memory now. I would still recognize them if I saw them today, however. I grieved their lost young lives. On three occasions I was chosen as a pall bearer for the funeral, slowly carrying my buddies to their final resting place under the heavily armored, watchful eyes of evil guards. We'd say a few words at the graveside and back we went.

As Air Force personnel we were accustomed to structure. Along with the camp's government, each prisoner had assigned jobs. Somehow, the camp acquired a collection of old books in English. It must have been another negotiated privilege. In a small unused corner section in one of the barracks we built a library.

A friend of mine from Connecticut was a book binder in civilian life. He took on the task of managing the library and preserving the books so they would last. The Germans gave him a small amount of supplies, including glue and paper to fix the bindings. I got to know him every well. Finally he said, "Do you want to help me?"

"Sure, I will."

Becoming an assistant book binder was my job in the prison camp. The fragile age of the books caused them to easily fall apart in sections, along the stitched bindings. We would put new sheets and covers on them and glue the books back together. It gave us something to do. We were able to keep the books in decent shape for a while. In fact, I still own the small wooden-handed knife I used in camp to repair those books.

Fellows read, but I don't know how well circulated the library was. I was mostly concerned with preventing the books from falling apart.

Most of the time, fellows played poker and card games. That's when I learned to play bridge. There were some great bridge players in the prison camp. It was competitive and we learned from each other. I loved it. I've only played bridge twice since camp and still miss it. We also played poker, using cigarettes for money. That's how we passed the time away.

One day toward the middle of the war, we heard a familiar roar overhead and ran into the compound, straining our eyes toward the distant sky. Two American planes flew overhead and buzzed around the camp. They knew we were there. They could see our faces. Hope is hard to hold on to in a prison camp, but, for a great long moment we clutched to the hope that we would be rescued soon.

Another time the Americans were on a bombing mission to Krems when they buzzed us again. A lead plane came and dropped orange flares around our camp. The whole place was lit up. They lit up the camp so the approaching pilots knew it was us and that our prison camp wasn't to be touched. We could hear the planes approaching. By the time they buzzed us their bomb bay doors were already open, bracing for the drop. We could see the bombs inside their planes. Minutes later we saw them dropping. We knew they were bombing the capitol. We were extremely fortunate that we were not bombed out that day.

After that day the Allied troops bombed the area fairly often. They would buzz our camp on the way to bombing Vienna, Krems and other cities. Our base was on the approach. As they came overhead the bomb bay doors were already open and they gave us a look inside. We could see the entire bomb load. It was their little signal telling us they were fighting for us. We just had to stay strong until we were liberated.

>Letter home - Oct. 25, 1944
>Gefangenennummer: 99959
>*Dear Mom,*
>*I received two letters from you three days ago. One from Al Swaczy and Anna. Your letters were dated June 9th and 15th. I'm glad to hear that everything is fine. I'm feeling swell and I'm getting along OK. I'm still working, reading and sleeping. Nothing else to do here. I wasn't sure whether Betty was going to school yet or not. Maybe she will be writing me letters soon. How are Pat, Tommy and Mitch making out? Did any of my stuff come home besides my rosary beads? In the next parcel you send, please put in a pair of rosary beads for me. I haven't had any with me. Do you get my allotment? Use whatever you want of it. Fred Holt, Baer and Gattman are all getting along OK too. That's all for now Mom. So I close. Say hello to all my friends for me.*
>*Love your son,*
>*Jerry*

Coupled with our daily BBC news reports and sightings of American bombers we knew the allied troops were getting close and we were winning the War. Boy, did we start giving the German guards a hard time. Out came our American sense of humor. It started with the morning roll call. In the beginning, the Germans would come into our barracks for roll call, yelling, "Macht schnell." If you didn't hurry fast enough you got a rifle butt. And it hurt! No matter the weather, the Germans lined us up outside for roll call and dog tag checks three or four times a day. They counted us in groups by barracks.

The Germans always counted the prisoners twice. I was always in the front of the line, so I didn't see the action. In the back a short guy would stand on the feet of a taller soldier and hide under his overcoat. That caused them to be short in their head count. Other times fellows would switch lines in mid count, causing the head count to be one extra. The Germans couldn't understand why their count was off, so they would count again. Then they would get the right answer. They'd want to count again and then would come up short again. This infuriated the German guards. They simply could not understand why Americans would want to play tricks on them.

Depending on the grief we gave them playing tricks, we would be standing in line for one to three hours at a time. Sometimes all day long. To our great delight, the amount of tricks escalated as we got closer to the end of the War.

Another time the guards discovered that we had an extra person in our ranks. He was an Englishman, who snuck in from another compound. They couldn't find him. They kept us outside in the lineup all day while they tore the barracks apart. They looked inside and out, under the cots and everything. The Germans never found him. We had him hidden in the water tank, which didn't have a proper fitting lid on the top. He was hanging onto the foot holds inside the tank, just above the waterline. Eventually, he was freed with us too. It was great.

I only had two full showers the entire time I was in the prison camp. To get to the showers we were marched in a group by barracks to a building just outside of the prison camp fence. The guards surrounded us in droves so that we couldn't escape. The Germans called the showers delousing. They used delousing to rid the camp of bugs and lice. They first shaved our heads. We were allotted a small amount of water. We had to soap up quickly and then had only three to five minutes to rinse everything off under the showers. The showering process was quick, but it took a few hours for everyone in our barracks to get deloused. The second time they took us for delousing we knew it was toward the end of the war. We didn't want them to shave our heads. Someone told us to put sand in our hair, which broke all their clippers. Boy, were they real angry at us. That was one of our biggest thrills.

The prisoners, we were all very friendly to each other. We stuck up for one another in Stalag XVIIB, no question about that. That's how we survived.

Letter from Home - Dec. 26, 1944

Dear Jerry,

We are all fine and hope to hear the same from you. Well Jerry as you know yesterday was Christmas. We all missed you. Our thoughts were with you all day. Let's hope that you will be with us next year. I hope you got some of our packages and letters before Christmas. We had some snow last week and it's been pretty cold lately. Betty likes the snow and was sleigh riding in front of the house. She looks so cute running up and down. She sends a big hug and a kiss. All the neighbors send their regards. Mom and Pop send their love. They said to keep you chin up always. Write when you can. Love all of us.

Love, Mom

(The letter was written by my sister Lucy for my mother.)

Chapter 10

THE DEATH MARCH

By the first week of April 1945 we knew something was up in the camp. Suddenly health and wellness inspections were being done in each compound. The guards tried to make us believe that after 19 months of torture they were trying to improve the conditions for us. Big brass suddenly showed up for tours and a new German captain was assigned to the camp, who spoke in scripted propaganda.

There was a nervous anxious energy that elevated. We weren't sure what was going to happen to us. Our daily radio broadcasts - "Gen" as we called it for general news - reported that the Allies were pushing closer to Berlin. The Germans had tried to attack Russia and take over the country, but the United States supplied Russia with planes and equipment. When the Russians got to Berlin, the German guards became fearful, because of what they had done in Russia. They didn't want to give up to the Russians. They certainly didn't want to stay around camp for fear that they would be killed in front of a band of American POWs.

As the Soviet Army was advancing, German authorities decided to evacuate POW camps, to delay liberation of the prisoners. In the later stages of the War there were great concerns among POWs over the motives for moving them westward. Many different and conflicting rumors abounded, including suggestions that they were being moved toward concentration camps to be killed, or force-marched until their deaths from exhaustion or held hostage to leverage peace deals. In

April 1945, the Germans ordered prisoners in Stalag XVIIB to make a two-week forced march to a small encampment near the town of Braunau, Austria.

By April 5, our Man of Command, the camp leader, spread the word that we needed to be prepared to evacuate. Ben H. Phelper noted in his book Kriegie Memories that it was rumored that the Russians were about 18 miles away from Krems, driving on St. Polten. We figured they would capture us in about three days. We knew they were close, because we could hear gunfire and could see big guns flashing at night. After lights out, it was like watching a lightening storm.

There were bonfires at night throughout the camp and anyone who had anything to trade suddenly became a business man.

As the morning dawned on April 8 the guards burst into our barracks yelling, "Pack up. Pack up. We're leaving in a little while." I believe the guards were as clueless as we were about the evacuation plan until they were actually ordered to leave camp.

We packed up everything we owned or could carry, rolling it into the one worn wool blanket on our beds. We carried our bedrolls like a backpack slung over our shoulders. Nothing of use or value was left behind. I didn't have too much: a few letters from home, my small bookbinding knife and a Certificate of Merit I earned for completing a 13-week course in algebra while in the camp school. I may have had another one for completing a course in French, too. The Germans already had a big piece of my life, my youth. I wasn't going to leave behind any evidence of the very life I cherished. That was all mine and I was keeping it. I put on every item of clothing I had and grabbed the overcoat given to me from the Red Cross. Somewhere along the way after I was shot down on Black Thursday, I lost my bomber jacket.

The guards broke us up in groups of 500 and marched us out of the prison camp by midday. The only people remaining in the camp were those who were unable to walk. I heard they spent April in the air raid tunnels. We, however, were told we needed to get to Innsbruck, which was about a 500 mile journey on foot, because Americans were on the other side of the river.

It took us three weeks to travel about 290 miles.

As we marched out of the prison camp we filed along the fence, passing the Russian camp. The Germans didn't give them a thing, not a blessed thing. We saw that. They just let them starve to death. Some were shot. Those who were strong enough to march were tortured even more. Every so often we would see them lying on the ground dead. The Germans didn't do anything for them. They were worse off than we were.

THE DEATH MARCH

That trek was so tough on me. I was so weak. I was emaciated by the time we left the prison camp: just 98 pounds. I don't know how I made it. I did it, but I had to do it. I had no other choice, but to go along and find ways to survive.

The first night we had nowhere to sleep. So, we just laid on the ground and placed our wool blankets over our heads.

We marched with a few miles between each group of 500 men. Sometimes a group would slow down, allowing a rear group to catch up. After a few days our physical condition began to show as guys started passing out along the way. We would hike for fifty minutes and rest for ten. Our group steadily strung out during the day. If you marched up front you could get a longer break until the guys in the back caught up. It was hard to stay up front though.

During the rest periods we ate, slept, talked or just stretched out. If there was any Gen to report, some fellow with lots of pep was assigned to read it off.

I don't believe the eight groups always took the same path. Ben Phelper did a great job of documenting the day-to-day details of the march in Kreigie Memories. Some of his stopover locations differ from mine, however. I do remember traveling dozens of miles in hilly or uneven terrain. I remember my weak blistered feet. The occasional break at a cold stream was my only medicine.

We were in poor shape. A lot of guys had been, like me, there for a year and a half. We weren't in good physical shape. We had to stop every so often to rest up. The guards knew it, but they kept us going as long as they could until we really complained. It was tough. It made for easy sleeping at night, even on the cold spring ground.

It was clear the Germans didn't know where they would stop at night or how they would feed us. At night we slept on the ground or in a barn, if we found one. Sometimes when we woke up the morning dew soaked our blankets. Supplying us with wood for fires wasn't even considered in the plan. As such, we became scavengers along the route. Even water was scarce.

We were fed a bowl of soup every two or three days, more if the Germans could confiscate something from locals as we crossed through a town. Along the way the local civilians had been good to the troops, giving us food or trading with us if they had anything, which wasn't much. Some guys traded cigarettes and chocolate with locals for an ax or a cart to carry things.

At this one place where we stopped for lunch, we walked up the road and saw a horse carcass next to the metal soup cart, a golf cart-sized vat on two wheels. So we knew it was horse soup, but it tasted good. Everything tasted good then. We had no food.

My experiences along the route are memories that fade in and out. I'd like to remember everything, but some are still best forgotten. I plodded along trying to survive.

The German guards also had little food or supplies. The stress of a three-week hike was taking its toll on several of them, as well. We saw German solders lying along the road dead.

We marched through one town in Austria where we stopped and handed out cigarettes in exchange for bread. That was so generous. People gave us bread. They knew we were starving.

Another day we went through a town where the villagers hated us, because we bombed them. That happened frequently as we wound through bombed out communities. I don't blame them for hating us. It was our job and we did it.

In mid-April we marched through one town covered by S.S. troops that had hell in their eyes, as Ben Phelper described it. Even the German guards were terrified of them. We moved as quickly as we could to get out of there.

Another night we slept on an island between two creeks. One creek was higher than the other, which meant that some of us woke up wet again. We hiked for several days along the Danube River before the Germans marched us across the mountains again. Our death march took us on a northwestern trek across the country.

Every night the boys with the homemade radios strung out their wires and listened for the BBC broadcasts. Radios were strictly forbidden by the guards. When we left camp, however, several radio sets went with us. It's funny looking back now on this one bit of vital communication. While we were in camp the guards frequently tore apart our barracks looking for radios and antennas. On the march, however, they did little to stop us from getting the news, either along the way or from the radios.

We ran through Linz, because the locals there hated us. We bombed them. There were a few incidents between the locals and members of the groups.

In the last few days of April, we arrived at the fork of the Inns and Salzach rivers with nothing to eat and nowhere to sleep. No shelter whatsoever. When we got there we could hear shooting across the Inns River and we knew the Americans were over there. The bridges had been blown up, however. We stumbled and labored down the last long hill before reaching Braunau am Inn, Austria, which is the birthplace of Adolph Hitler. There they pushed us into the dense woods.

We immediately began to establish our own camp sites. Other groups were already building there. Most of the fellows made huts out of branches and any ropes or wires they had. The few who were able to trade for axes began chopping down trees and building log cabins that were used for sick bays, supply huts and quarters. They covered the roofs with tree branches and moss, which still leaked after it rained. To stay warm they built fires inside the cabins, which unfortunately caused a few to catch fire. Others built elaborate teepees. A team dug slit trenches for latrines, lining them with tree trunks for seats. It wasn't easy to establish a camp. We were scrounging. There were maybe six or seven axes for 4,000 POWs. Anytime I asked to borrow one I was told another fellow got it next and there was long waiting list. If I ever did get my hands on one it was only for few minutes. Oftentimes, the guards scoffed at the amount of barkless trees.

Again, I grabbed a few tree branches and made my space with my wool blanket in a lean-to with a couple of buddies. I will never forget waking up on May 2 covered in two inches of snow. It melted quickly.

Water was our first need. We were already existing without food, but we couldn't survive without water. To get it we had to climb down an extremely long, steep hill from the camp toward the river without ropes, paths or help. About halfway down the hill there was a terrace where we stopped to rest. I had to. The water was cold, deep and green. We didn't bathe in it for fear of being swept away. We used whatever bottles and cans we had to carry water back to the camp site. I didn't really have any good cans. On the way back up the hill I lost half my water. It took two to three hours to climb down and back. Man, was that tough. We had to take turns doing that.

While positioned in the woods, we could hear the sustained shooting across the Inns River. We knew our troops couldn't get to us, however, because the bridges were destroyed. It took American troops a few days to build bridges and bring their equipment across the river to us.

As the Americans got closer, the Germans became leery. Finally, they just took off. They changed out of their military uniforms and put on civilian clothes, as if they were never in the service. They were gone a couple of days and we didn't even know it.

On May 3 I was standing on a bluff above the river watching American tanks and jeeps moving on the other side, just as the sun was setting at about 6:30 p.m., when an Army captain and a driver strode up the road. We told him we were POWs.

"Well, you're no longer POWs. You're free! You can go into town if you'd like," he said as the woods erupted into wild cheering. The captain was part of the U.S. 13th Armored and the 80th Infantry Divisions.

Physically we were near death. Emotionally we were overwhelmed. We finally had permission to freely entertain the thought that we would be recused. At that very moment, when the captain drove up in a Jeep with his soldier and said we were freed, I felt fairly confident that we were going to go home. All those feelings I thought - all those dreams I had about coming home to my family in Chatham, about the safety of home - were about to come true. It was an amazing rush of emotions. We were getting out of there.

The next day I went into town with my buddies. There were American soldiers bivouacked in a building in town. When they found out we were POWs they called us in and fed us. They fed us everything - juice, bacon, eggs, hams, bagels. The smell alone of real food cooking in a house was filling. We ate everything they gave us. I never stopped eating. They fed us so much that, when we came out of the building, I heaved everything up. Our stomachs had shrunk so much that our bodies couldn't take it. It sure felt good going down, though.

That was a perfectly good waste of meat. We could have used half of that during our time in prison camp. It felt good to eat it all and we were very thankful to the soldiers. They knew it, too.

Hitler's army had surrendered prior to my leaving the camp in Braunau, along the German-Austrian border, about 55 miles from Linz and 36 miles north of Salzburg.

We were taken across a river to an airport. It was like a hanger. It was there that we were freed for a couple of days. That's where we found a German supply barracks with bayonets, rifles and stuff lying around. We took whatever we wanted. So I took a couple of knives. A couple of guys took home brand new German rifles. Today they're worth a few hundred dollars. I didn't, because I didn't think we could get them through security. We had to register any nonmilitary possessions. They told us we couldn't take them home. I took two bayonets, which I buried deep in my barracks bag.

> The Royal Air Force Bomber Command implemented Operation Exodus from RAF Oakley air base and the first prisoners of war were repatriated by air on May 2, 1945. The RAF Bomber Command flew 2,900 sorties over the next 23 days, carrying 72,500 prisoners of war. RAF Oakley was a three-runway airfield between Oakley and Worminghall, Buckinghamshire. For many veterans, the base with its flat, damp wooded surroundings will forever be remembered as the soil of freedom.

THE DEATH MARCH

When I got out of there and they flew us to Camp Lucky Strike in Le Havre, France I weighed 98 pounds. I was so malnourished that I couldn't make the trip home for three weeks. Most of us were there for the same reasons.

> After the Allies secured the French harbor of Le Havre, on the eastern side of the Bay of Seine, the Americans began ringing the city with camps that served as staging areas for new troops arriving in the European Theater of Operations (ETO). Eight tent cities were established in farm fields along the northern coast of France, between Le Havre and Rouen. Named after popular cigarette brands, the camps were hastily erected conglomerations of tents and wooden huts. These sprawling tent cities were rather primitive places characterized by a sense of transience with little if any conveniences. Camp Lucky Strike, which was located between Cany-Barville and Saint-Valery, had a capacity for 58,000 soldiers. It was one of the largest camps. When the end of the war in Europe was in sight in 1945 these camps underwent tremendous changes, in anticipation for the role they would play in recovery and repatriation after the war was over. Barracks and other permanent structures were built, such as hospitals and a PX. Mess halls replaced outdoor chow lines at mobile field kitchens.
>
> It is estimated that nearly three million American troops either entered or left Europe through the cigarette camps at Le Havre, which led to it becoming known as the Gateway to America in 1945-46.

When I got to Camp Lucky Strike my entire group was assigned a bed in the hospital. It was a huge tent hospital in the middle of a big field, nearly the size of a football field. We were too weak to set up our own cots in our own tents.

There were tens of thousands of soldiers in camp. I don't know when Camp Lucky Strike was at its peak of 58,000 soldiers, but I'm certain it was after the war when all those POW camps and concentration camps were liberated. We were one of the last ones to be freed, because we were on the western part of the war zone. Many may have already moved through the camp on their way home, before we arrived.

The treatment they gave us slowly brought us back from near starvation. Our meals weren't piled high with hearty bacon and fried eggs every day, but they did give us food. The memories of those day-to-day moments in the cigarette camp have faded. A few details remain. We were told not to go out at night. The French weren't particularly happy. This was the second time we gave the French back their country and they still didn't like us. I never understood that. It was disappointing.

The one thing I do remember about my time in the camp is not a political statement, but rather a moment of disrespect from an authority.

The morning after we arrived at Camp Lucky Strike we were standing in the chow line. They were these huge winding lines with thousands of faces of hungry soldiers. We had arrived late the night before. Who comes up to us, but General Dwight Eisenhower. The gentleman behind me hadn't shaved. He couldn't, because he had no equipment. No razors. Eisenhower said, "Boy, what are you doing here? You're in the Army. You should be shaved." We never said a damn thing. I'm not making a political statement here, but I never liked Eisenhower from that point on. I didn't vote for him for president, because of that one statement. He should have known we had just gotten out of a POW camp. One of his people should have told him. I will never forget that. It was surprising. Why a man would do a thing like that? He's an officer, a general. But it happened.

There was a sign prominently displayed at Camp Lucky Strike that in no uncertain terms stated "personnel being processed through this camp were entitled to have one souvenir pistol in their possession. Anyone found to have more than one will be court marshaled and given a sentence of six months hard labor in the European Theater of Operations." The barrel outside the registration tent was stacked with discarded war souvenirs.

In the three weeks that I was recovering I was never asked to register any souvenir pistols or knives. I kept mum and stashed my bayonets in my barracks bag. I didn't do a particularly good job of hiding them, either. I just didn't register them. Some of the fellows had rifles that they had to turn them in. They were discovered.

I had time to think about all the possibilities for tomorrow and time to reflect on everything that happened. I could not have survived were it not for the soldiers' bond. We helped each other through every moment of every day. You see, the POWs couldn't help with anything. We didn't have anything: no food or stuff. We could only be friendly. That's all we could do. The Germans couldn't change that spirit in Americans.

THE DEATH MARCH

V-Mail Letter home - May 17, 1945
USAAF ID: 32461208
Approved by Censor - 1st Lt. D.C. Seaver - Camp Lucky Strike
To: Mrs. Carmela Caporaso,
61 Passaic Ave.
Chatham, N.J.

Dear Mom,
I imagine by now you have heard that I have been liberated. I am back in American hands now in France and waiting to be shipped home. I'll probably be on my way home by the time you receive this letter. We're getting good care and plenty of good food. Last night I met Lt. Kiernan and Lt. Malik. They came in the day before yesterday. Both of them are fine. Gattman, Baer and Holt. Although I haven't seen Gattman and Holt lately I know they are O.K. I hope everyone at home is getting along as well as we are. Tell Betty it won't be long before I will be home now. We'll probably be on our way home by the time you get this letter. Don't bother to write. I will try to call as soon as I can when we get in the states. I will see you soon.
Love your son,
Jerry

Chapter 11

COMING HOME

Our time in the European Theater of Operations was coming to a close. The United States began a mass exodus to ferry hundreds of thousands of tired, haggard and wounded soldiers back home. The post-war work was just beginning. It would be many months before the military could break down hospital tents at the cigarette camps dotting the northern French coast. They were transient communities. Everyone was friendly and extremely helpful, but faces came and went daily.

At 98 pounds, I could barely move when I arrived, let alone carry out any official duties. Slowly, day by day, I got my energy back. After three weeks the unfathomable became clear: I was going home. Home to American soil. Home to everything that was familiar and safe to me. For almost two years I could only dream about stepping foot onto the train station platform in Chatham and walking a few blocks home where the lilting scents of my mother's home cooking hypnotized me all the way up the slanted hill on South Passaic Avenue. Home is where one's story begins. Going home again after the war is where my story continued. That dream became reality, as if I had just won the greatest prize in the world: Life.

And I had.

Eventually, I was sent back home on a Victory ship overloaded with POWs. Walking onto the ship the first thing I noticed was that the deck was stacked high with wooden cots from one end to the other. It was so crowded with people trying to sleep on the decks. They were shipping home as many as they could. It was exciting in that we all knew we were coming home and it was also a boat trip. It was my first boat trip. After 19 months in a prison camp, three weeks of sleeping on the ground in Austria and another three weeks in a mobile hospital, the steely walls of this Victory ship looked like a floating four-star hotel to me. It was taking me where I needed to go. We left Le Havre, France on June 1.

There were 534 Victory ships built during World War II, according to a U.S. Merchant Marine website. They were named after Allied nations, American cities, educational institutions and several miscellaneous names. The attack transports were named after counties, except one named after President Franklin D. Roosevelt's personal secretary Marvin H. McIntyre. These floating powerhouses were 455 feet long and 62 feet wide. Their cross-compound steam turbines with double reduction gears could produce 6,000 to 8,500 horsepower. They were typically armed with one five-inch stern gun, one three-inch bow gun and eight 20 millimeter machine guns.

For the first time in a long time, I wished for something. I hoped I would be home by my birthday on June 15. The Victory ship had to zigzag its way across the Atlantic Ocean. There was fear that some of the Allied submarine pilots had not received the message that the war was over and would shoot us down. After a week on the water, we finally got the green light to travel straight into the New York harbor.

Seeing the New York skyline again was like seeing it for the first time, its architectural magnificence rising up out of the horizon as we pulled closer. It's energy drew us to the railings. People cheered us on as we pulled into port. I don't remember the weather, but it's always sunny when you return home from war. We arrived in the Port of New York on June 12. I got my wish.

> Totaling an area more than 1,200 square miles, New York harbor comprised more than 430 miles of water. During World War II, the harbor was divided into 600 individual ship anchorages able to accommodate ocean-going vessels awaiting berthing and already loaded and awaiting convoy assignments and sorties, according to data compiled by researchers at the New York State Museum.
>
> The Port of New York boasted a developed shoreline of over 650 miles comprising the waterfronts of Manhattan, Brooklyn, Queens, the Bronx, and Staten Island, as well as the New Jersey shoreline from Perth Amboy to Elizabeth, Bayonne, Newark, Jersey City,

COMING HOME

Hoboken and Weehawken. Between the bombing of Pearl Harbor on Dec. 7, 1941 and VJ-Day, which is officially Sept. 2, 1945, more than three million troops and their equipment and more than 63 million tons of materials and supplies were shipped overseas through the Port of New York.

There are certain moments that stand out and stay with you forever. We were weary and hungry and the first snafu happened right on the dock. As we filed off the ship, we walked passed rows of tables lined with fresh doughnuts and hot coffee being sold by Red Cross volunteers. That was our welcome home. We just came home from overseas on a boat. We had no food, no money, nothing. We couldn't even get a doughnut and a cup of brew for free. Yet, we had to walk past all those tables, staring, once again, at food we could not eat. It was hurtful. I will never forget that. I know the Red Cross did a lot of good during the War, but when we came home we were prisoners of war. It would have done the Red Cross a lot of good will to set up free tables. I have had no use for the organization since.

I couldn't go home right away. I was still serving in the Air Force officially. I don't even know if my parents knew I was back on home soil again. From New York we were sent down to a base in Atlantic City for a while to shape up a bit. From there they gave me a 60-day furlough and then extended it another two weeks while Air Force officials decided where to station me. I got to spend the summer in Chatham.

It was such a relief to be home and on vacation. I would have rather been out of the Air Force at that time, but it was OK. I was still getting paid to serve. When I got home my mother was at a friend's house. The family called her to come home. She took one look at me and could not believe how skinny I was. Every nurturing instinct of hers went into overdrive. She made it her personal mission to put weight on me in a hurry. I was very happy to be home.

After the United States dropped atomic bombs on Hiroshima and Nagasaki, Japan surrendered on August 14, 1945. My family, like every household in America, over celebrated. When World War II ended I was with my family and friends having a party at my house in Chatham! I had a little too much to drink that day.

Eventually I had to go back to work. To be discharged from the service a soldier had to accumulate more than 70 points. You were given a point for every month you served and two points for every month you served overseas. I was just shy of a release. When I returned home I had more than 65 points and for whatever reason the government didn't release prisoners of war right away. I still don't understand why they would not let us go. We were POWs: we weren't going to do anything. I reported back to the base in Atlantic City in late August where I was assigned to work at the Army Air Force base in Rome, New York.

My first assignment there was to participate in an Honor Guard in full dress uniform complete with white spats to welcome home General Jonathan Mayhew Wainwright from the Pacific.

General Wainwright was a second-generation career Army officer, who was the commander of the Allied forces in the Philippines at the time of their surrender to Japan. In the interest of minimizing casualties, General Wainwright surrendered when the Japanese attacked Corregidor on April 9, 1942. He was among the 70,000 troops serving on Bataan. He was held in several prison camps throughout the Philippines until his liberation by the Red Army in August 1945. He was the highest-ranking American POW and, despite his rank, his treatment at the hands of the Japanese was extremely rough. He was dubbed the fighting man's general for his willingness to climb down into foxholes. It has been said that while he agonized over feelings of letting his country down, he won the respect of all who were imprisoned with him. He later received the Metal of Honor. I suppose his trip to Rome, New York was his first stop back into the United States, as a giant ticker-tape parade was held in his honor in New York City on September 13, 1945. It was a big deal to me to be a part of the honor guard. I knew exactly how he felt stepping back onto U.S. soil in the company, safety and freedom of fellow soldiers. It felt wonderful to participate in something that important. Everything you once held dear you now held more closely.

I had a good time in Rome, but I didn't stay long. I met a nice Italian gal there, who took me home to meet her mother. When her mother found out I was a prisoner of war she started cooking for me.

I was reassigned to work at the airfield in Syracuse, New York. Because I was a master sergeant they weren't quite sure what duties to give me. I was assigned to manage all the Air Force fighting equipment: the parachutes, clothing, tools and stuff. I really didn't know the first thing about managing supplies. Pilots came in to pick up parachutes. Mechanics came in to get tools to fix the planes. Others came in to pick up those heavy leather bomber jackets. The men could have robbed me blind and I would not have known. If I knew then what I know now I would have shipped home some bomber jackets. I lost mine after we crashed on Black Thursday. When I came home I was issued new military clothing and another jacket. I still have it, even though I don't wear it anymore.

> Syracuse Air Force base was a 3,500-acre facility located north of the city with three 5,500-foot runways. The base was used as a

staging and storage area, repairing and re-outfitting the B-17 and B-24 aircraft that had been used during the war. After the war the base was converted to a commercial airfield.

Finally the order came to release all prisoners of war from active duty. I had 67 points, almost there anyway. My Honorable Discharge was processed at the Army Air Force base in Rome on November 7, 1945. I was given money to take a train to New York City, a ferry across the harbor to Jersey City and another train to Hoboken. I called the house and told my father I would be home in an hour or so. I was coming home for good.

As the train pulled into the Chatham station just off Main Street, I suddenly had a flashback to being a child and running along the tracks as trains pulled into town. The station with its elevated tracks was built in 1914, just seven years before I was born. As a child I remember all the steam engines rolling through town with their lofty billows of deep black smoke snake-charming the town as they pulled away, encouraging us to travel. It became a neighborhood ritual for a gaggle of kids, myself included, to tease the engineer to toss us bits of coal off the train that we could use in our coal stoves at home. They had fun lobbing handfuls of coal off the sides of the trains and watching us scamper for them, like rich prizes. The chunks were larger than a grown man's fist, larger than the typical pieces we had at the house. Sometimes I collected enough coal to fill a bucket, which was a day's worth of cooking coal for my Mom that I got for free.

I thought about how when the electric trains finally came through town the teachers at St. Patrick's took us on a walking field trip to the train station to welcome the new technology. Now I was coming home from war on one. The train jerked to a stop and woke me out of the daydream.

My father and the American Legion Commander Joe McNany were the only people waiting for me on the platform. Mr. McNany was also the assistant post master in town. It was so odd. Here soldiers were coming home from war and we were expecting bigger things than that really, but we didn't get it. No welcoming ceremonies, flag-waving parades or even a crowd of people. Dad and Mr. McNany were the only ones who knew I was coming home. My return was not as fanciful as one might think. That's fine. I was just happy to be home finally. It was wonderful to see Chatham again. Dad and Mr. McNany wanted to take me out to dinner, but I said I've got to home to see Mom. She had a big meal waiting for me.

My mother kept feeding me and feeding me. For weeks there was a steady stream of ham, spaghetti and meatballs, vegetables, potatoes and my favorite,

Easter meat pie. To my benefit I arrived after the fall harvest when the last prizes of Dad's fruitful gardens were picked, stored and canned for the winter.

I didn't work for a whole year. I just wasn't ready. I was too weak. No one could rush the time I needed to get my head together, to think like a civilian and not like a scavenger or, even, to feel comfortable walking around a free man again. A prisoner of war is always haunted by moments that just reappear unexpectedly.

During that time I didn't do very much. When my brother, Tommy came home from the war we played cards and golf a few times. We were treated to free golf in Florham Park. Tommy was in the Medical Corps and served in Africa for a long time before being reassigned to Italy. While there he got to meet relatives in Naples and took care of them with food and supplies. My brother John served in the Navy on the USS Randolph. Carmen, who we called Mitchell, was a B-17 gunner flying in the Pacific, but didn't see much combat. One morning he was supposed to fly a mission, but woke up with a hernia and had to be replaced. That day his plane crashed and the entire crew was lost. Two brothers were already married when I came home: so I didn't see them too often. Together we talked a little bit about our war experiences, a sort of a family therapy, but we tried not to talk too much about it. It was best to live it forward. There were so many fellows, who didn't get to come home. We didn't want to dwell on the negative past.

One of my neighbors, who lived a few homes away on the next street, finally approached me and said, "You've got to get a job. Do you want to work for Mr. Brocci?" He designed and built awnings for homes and businesses and needed a helper. I didn't know what else to do. So I went to work for Mr. Bocci earning $40 a week, which was good money at the time. I learned to sew and install awnings.

After a year a postman I knew well told me that the U.S. Postal Service was hosting the federal Post Office entrance exam. I didn't want to stay in the awning business for the rest of my career, so I took the exam and finished second. I was a quarter of a point behind the leader. Both of us were POWs and master sergeants. Thank goodness the Postal Service was short handed. We were both hired quickly. The post master knew I was a local boy and that I attended Catholic school with his children. I began working there in 1947 and retired as Chatham's assistant postmaster 42 years later.

Over the years I was offered three appointments as post master in other towns, but I didn't want them. I didn't want to travel out of town. I was satisfied with working in Chatham, no matter what pay raise was offered to me to leave. I knew the town, the routines, the mail routes and the habits of a community. When I started working in the post office there were 3,000 people living in Chatham. Now there are 10,000 residents.

There was an issue of money that needed to be settled after I returned from war. I had been a prisoner of war for 19 months, technically working on flying pay. I also received my promotion to master sergeant while I was in the prison camp. The Army had to catch up with me.

When I entered the service I arranged for a $75 allotment to be sent home to my mother each month. With small children still at home I wanted her to have extra money. It was the working rule of a big family: some goes to the house. When I was first drafted I was making $20 a month. Shortly after that the Air Force raised the pay to $30 a month for a private. When I became a staff sergeant my pay was raised to $96 a month and as a technical sergeant I earned $114 a month. Additionally, we were paid fifty percent more for flying four hours a month. That was flying pay or mission pay. It didn't take long to total up. The $96 a month salary, quickly became $144 and the $114 jumped to $171 after four hours in the air. I found out my mother never spent a dime of the money that was sent to her. She stashed away several thousand dollars for me. I tried to insist that she keep it, but she wanted me to have it.

The first two years I was home I was still trying to figure out what I was owed. I had back pay and back promotional pay, because I was promoted from a tech sergeant to a master sergeant while I was in the prison camp, which earned a base salary of $138 a month. I got flying pay, an extra payment for being a prison of war, and a payment for the length of time I was a POW. That was a pretty good payday. When all was settled I had thousands of dollars in the bank and a new job I loved in Chatham.

I treated myself to some wheels. A friend of mine in the post office ordered two brand new cars, a Chevy and another one. He ultimately liked the other one better. So I bought the Chevy from him for $2,000. As a matter of fact I gave him a $50 tip for making the arrangements for me. I had that car a long time.

I joined the Chatham Fire Department in 1947, officially its 50th anniversary year. I've now seen it through the 75th and 100th anniversaries.

It's a funny thing how my love of baseball led to my other family, my fire house family. The Chatham Fire Department started a softball league among other fire departments in the area. I was a manager of a softball team in Chatham at the time. One day a fellow I knew gave me a ride in his truck and asked me to join the fire department so that I could play on its team. That's what got me there.

The fire house family is the reason I stayed. There was some training, but not as intensive as new members have today. I was taught how to work the equipment and manage fires as I went along. At the time Chatham was only partially built up. We mostly fought brush fires: lawns, fields and stuff. Often the ash or burning coals from steam engines rolling through town would ignite the fields alongside the tracks and spread quickly. I learned to fight fires by carrying a spray tank on my back and putting out brush fires manually. We had brooms that we also used to sweep out the flames. I only attended a few house fires when I was younger. We didn't have too many in those days. Houses were different back then. There weren't the furnishings and chemicals that exist in homes today.

I'm still an active member, but I don't fight fires anymore. In a fire department there are many different types of jobs for members, besides fighting fires. I was elected secretary and treasurer and served as lieutenant and captain of the Chatham Hose Company. From the 1950's until about 2005, I served as parade chairman. I was secretary of the Firemen's General Relief Fund for more than forty years. We had picnics and dances for our wives and trout-stocked fishing derbies for the kids on the pond. We always had something going on.

Still, you get into a routine at home. When you go to bed at night you know where everything is in the house, just in case you get called out for an emergency. When I was newly married and living in a garage apartment on South Passaic Avenue, across the street from my parent's house, I was only two blocks away from the fire house. My clothing was always right by the bed. Several times I went out in the middle of the night, all ready to go, and I would be the first person to arrive at the fire house.

One of my early fires happened just after midnight on Christmas Eve. The Chatham Fish and Game Protective Association men's club, just down the street on Fairmount Avenue, caught fire. It was cold as heck. Two fellows, Dick and Skip Conlin, and I were the first people to arrive at the fire house. Dick and I had the hose on the fire and Skip was on the truck taking care of the pumper until more people and the Red Cross showed up. The house was all wood and burned straight to the ground like kindling.

The thing about being a firefighter is that every fire is a notorious fire to someone. Something in town is now gone. We work to keep the residents safe.

Chapter 12

MY VIRGINIA

After the war, money was scarce. We were still pulling out of the Great Depression and not too many people had jobs. When it came to having fun we had to be resourceful. Between my sisters' friends and my friends, our house became a continuous hub of social activity. Someone was always eating at my house. We went on group dates on the weekends to the movies or out into town. We weren't dating as single dates. It was more like a pile of people doing something together. So I knew my wife long before we ever went out on a date.

Virginia was best friends with my sister Virginia. They were always together, like giggling book ends. We called them both Ginny. I could still see my Virginia standing in our family's kitchen, a slender 5'5" with a head of curly blonde ringlets.

Eventually, we paired off a little bit and cut down on the size of the group date. My friend Jack Spencer and I had our dates together. That's when Virginia and I started dating. It's amazing, but we never had a particular thing: no one big wow moment of dating like some people do. It just worked into it.

Virginia had interviewed to be an airline hostess and was turned down. She wasn't too upset about it, but the thought of traveling the world together was briefly exciting to me. Instead she worked at a bank in town for many years.

We started discussing marriage after a while. I met her mother and father, Margaret and Charles Stanek, and knew them well. Virginia had a sister and a brother.

I'll never forget the first time I brought Virginia's parents home for a formal dinner to meet my parents. Because she was from a small family everything they did or ate was done on a smaller scale. In one shot they met the whole Caporaso family. On occasions like this my mother always cooked ham and salad for the first plate. The Stanek's ate that with great delight and waited for desert. When my mother brought out a great big bowl of spaghetti they were amazed. Their eyes stretched to the size of golf balls. They couldn't get over it. My mother was always like that. She fed a crowd every day. As such she never cooked just one thing on a special occasion. We would have ham, chicken, spaghetti and meatballs. The platters kept getting passed. Oh, do I miss those days.

Virginia wanted to get married on a particular day in August. I agreed. Jack threw a monkey wrench into our plans, however, when he announced he was getting married on the same week. Virginia was a little angry when I told her we couldn't get married.

"Why do I have to wait for Jack to get back," she insisted?

"Because I am in the wedding party."

It wasn't that bad of an argument.

We got married a few weeks later on September 1, 1951. I'll never forget my wedding day. Weddings back then were just as much fun, but far more simple than they are today. We got married at St. Patrick's chapel and the entire wedding reception was held at my in-law's house on Watchung Avenue. I was friendly with the fire chief at the time. He brought the fire engine over to my in-law's house and gave us a ride around town. You can't do that anymore, because they don't let untrained people on the trucks. My favorite wedding photo is of us standing on the back of the fire truck.

When we were first married we rented a tiny one-bedroom apartment above the shop at a greenhouse on Watchung Avenue, across the street and up a block from where my wife lived. We had friends who lived there and moved out. It was hard to find any apartment available in Chatham at the time. We had looked for apartments and couldn't find any others, so we took it. We stayed there about a year when a larger garage apartment became available across the street from my parent's house. We knew the gentleman owner, Charles Miller. My father used to give him tomato plants. Another year into our marriage we began looking for a home of our own.

Houses in Chatham were expensive. Everyone wanted a great deal of money. We went into one home on Washington Avenue and asked if it had a basement. The owner said yes and started to take us downstairs. I had to duck my head to get down there. It was more like a wine cellar, the ceiling was so low. They wanted quite a bit of money for the house, too: maybe $35,000. We weren't having any of that. We looked at new houses and old houses, all expensive houses. We weren't finding anything in Chatham we liked within our price range.

The beginning of the baby boom had started. Soldiers, like me, returning from war were setting down roots and starting families. There was a dire need for new housing in this country. Eventually we noticed a new neighborhood was being built in Summit. The three different model homes were constructed at the end of Canoe Brook Parkway, each priced at $19,900. We liked what they offered and bought one.

With my Virginia, my American dream started in a three-bedroom split level on a corner lot at 1 Sheridan Rd in Summit. I took all my back pay from surviving being a POW in the war and put $10,000 down on the home. Buying your first home is a victorious enough accomplishment. It felt more magnificent to walk my bride across the threshold and whispered to myself, "I didn't let the enemy win."

When we went to Summit Bank to apply for a mortgage the banker told us with delight that he could give us a loan with a five percent interest rate.

"Not for me. I'm putting down a $10,000 deposit on a $20,000 house and you want to charge me the going rate of five percent. I won't pay more than four percent interest."

"Oh, we can't do that," he said.

"Ok," I said, "I'll go someplace else." I started walking out the door when the banker came running after me.

"Wait. Let me talk to the boss."

He went into the back room and after a long while came back with an offer of four and a half percent.

I said, "No. That's not going to work. I want four percent or I won't buy a mortgage from you."

So he went back again. Aaaaah, he wasn't talking to anyone. It was one of those things. Sure enough, he came back and said, "All right, you can have a mortgage for four percent."

Since we were paying for half the house up front, I figured we deserved a special rate. If we went bankrupt the bank would still have a good deal and a new house. Our initial mortgage payments, which included the real estate taxes, were $67 a month. Eventually we paid it off.

Split level houses were a new model of family friendly homes. You could be on one floor and keep track of the children on any level of the house. We watched this home being built. After our boys were born it became the secondary park in the neighborhood as they were always organizing a soccer match, baseball game or a round of basketball in the back yard with their friends. With a corner lot we had more room to play. Like my home growing up there was always a cluster of children in the yard. The home plate for baseball was on the side corner of the back yard, closest to the house. If the boys hit the ball over the neighbor's fence it was considered a home run. The dining room used to have a window that overlooked the backyard action. We lost a few panes of glass on occasion. Virginia and I loved being the neighborhood kid depot, the flop house of children playing together. That's the way we liked it.

These are some of my favorite memories of our home. They are reminders of a life well lived. We're still laughing and retelling these shared memories in our own words. That's what makes them fun. They are our life story.

The first family to be our back-yard neighbors, the Waters, bought the corner lot on Beverly Road and installed an in-ground pool. We were very friendly with them and they couldn't do enough for my boys. They allowed them to swim in their pool whenever they wanted. They were allowed to bring friends too, as long as nothing was destroyed. As you can figure, in the steamy summer days the boys lived there.

One of the funniest stories came out of that open-door policy. When we built this house we had a fourth bedroom built downstairs on the side of the recreation room. As Jim got older he decided he wanted that space for his own room. That also allowed Steve and Bob to have their own rooms. Mr. Waters once told me that after the pool was opened in the spring, Jim would come over every morning to swim a few laps before heading off to high school. I didn't know a thing about it.

We started our own family traditions. Christmas celebrations were rotated between our house, and those of Virginia's sister, Margaret, and her brother, Bill. My youngest sister, Betty, joined us too. Now that our children are grown and have their own homes we're still circulating between houses.

Betty worked as a supervisor for the Chubb Corporation. When the company needed some temporary help in the office, Virginia went back to work. She took several assignments there before they offered her a full-time job. One of our dreams was to be able to put our three sons through college without them incurring any debt. While I earned a decent living at the post office it was Virginia's work at Chubb that helped us realize that dream. That was something we were both very proud of and we know our sons are grateful.

I could retell stories about my boys forever. They make me smile.

The Little League baseball program started in the surrounding Chatham area when I was a kid. As such, when the boys were young I became involved in the organization in Summit as soon as we registered them. League organizers urged me to get involved, because they desperately needed active parents. I had volunteered as an umpire with girls softball leagues before and they urged me to umpire again. Whenever there was a tough game scheduled the League officials always assigned me to umpire. It became quite a bit after a while. I liked it, but they didn't have many other umpires. I was the only one for a long time until they finally recruited a few parents for me to train. We all got along quite well.

One season I became a manager for Steve's team. That was the same year he made the All-Star team. Coaches voted for players from each team to participate on the All-Star team. A father couldn't vote for his own child. Steve thought I did, but that wasn't the case. The other managers selected him.

The story we retell constantly, reliving the glory days of Little League, was the year Steve played in the League championships at Summit High School when he was about 12 years old. His team played well all season and progressed to the championship game. He had never pitched before. He came to me and asked, "What should I do? What should I play?" Steve liked to be in the middle of the action all the time. I suggested he either pitch, catch or play first base. He was a bit hesitant about pitching, because he had never done it before. So I took him out a few times and showed him how to pitch. To his advantage, Steve was a pretty good size for himself and could throw a fast ball. Children that age, playing against a bigger pitcher with a fast ball, tend to back away. Steve did well. He pitched only one game.

The team puts the weakest player in right field. It's very seldom that the ball goes to right field. In the championship game, however, a player belted one to right field in the second inning. It streamed passed the right fielder and a fellow ran around Steve for a home run. The rest of the innings plodded along. In the ninth inning, Steve got up to bat last. From behind the plate I was secretly hoping he got a home run or, at least, a decent base hit. I was behind home plate as an umpire, however, and I had to do my job. He swung at two good pitches and missed them twice. As the opposing pitcher was winding up I remember looking at his little face and glancing over at my son and thinking, "Come on, Steve, hit it over the fence." The ball came in perfectly and, as the familiar whomp of a baseball landing in the hallow of the catcher's leather mitt echoed across the field, I was torn at that moment between sounding like a Dad and being an umpire. I struck him out and the game ended 1-0.

The other parents were shocked. They found it incredulous that I would even consider striking out my own son. I simply told them that I called the game the way I saw it. He deserved to be struck out. I knew there wasn't anything wrong with it. Steve didn't get angry at me, either. After the game I told him he pitched a really good game. Bob and Steve and their friends still talk about it.

It's funny how one little piece of advice can entirely change your direction in sports. Jim wanted to play football in junior high school. When my wife took him to get a sports physical the doctor advised him not to play football.

"You don't want to play football. You've got something wrong with your back," the doctor said. "If someone hits you hard you're liable to wreck your back." He accepted it, even though it upset him.

When I was in school Chatham High School didn't have a football program. The school had a program years earlier, but cancelled it after a player broke his neck. That's when the football coach switched sports and began laying the foundation for a decades long soccer legacy in the Chatham. The team often played larger schools and won a number of state championships. I reminded Jim about that.

At first he didn't want to play soccer. I reminded him that soccer is more demanding than football, because you are running all the time and have to be in excellent shape. With football, you have to be strong, but you are only moving for moments at a time.

Fortunately for him, Jim's first coach was a good coach. When he came home he said, "You're right about it being tough, Dad." He followed that coach, Lou DiParisi, to high school. And so began our soccer legacy. Jim's playing experience encouraged Steve and Bob to play soccer, too. They all played wearing number eight on their uniform.

In Jim's senior year, his third season under coach Lou DiParisi, Summit High School won its first ever Suburban Conference Soccer Championship in the fall of 1974 and then went on to capture the New Jersey Interscholastic Athletic Association Group 3 State Championship, 2 -1, over Ewing Township. With the score tied 1-1 late in the second half Summit was awarded a free kick from 40 yards out. It was a cold November day, but most in the crowd of 5000 people were standing up yelling and screaming for their team. Doug Colson lofted a perfect cross towards the far post. Jimmy was the target. I don't know how he got so high in the air. He bolted straight up and headed that long free kick from his friend Doug back across the box directly to Matt Bowyer, who hammered the ball into the back of the net from ten yards out. That's how they won the State Championship. It was Summit's winningest season ever, dating back to 1938, with a final record of 18-2-2. The University of North Carolina recruited Jimmy during that tournament and soccer has remained an important part of his life to this day.

In Steve's senior year, his soccer team went 17-4-5 and was NJSIAA Group III co-champions with Steinert High School in Mercer County. The two schools tied the final game, 0-0. Unfortunately, Summit did not repeat as the Suburban Conference champions that year.

Those were good times. Soccer was new for us and so was the program at Summit under Coach DiParisi. In his first four years heading the high school program, from 1973 to 1976, Coach DiParisi set a four-year record of 54 wins, 18 losses and nine ties that included three championship titles. We were a part of that dynasty.

Boy Scouts was another tradition. As legions of young boys were taught leadership and team-building skills, my sons loved the build-it competitions.

When Steve was in Cub Scouts, the troop held a rocket competition. The boys were given packets with a block of balsam wood with predrilled holes, a rubber band, propeller, a few pieces of wire and a tail section, and told to build and paint their own rockets. Steve brought his rocket home and painted the nose red, the middle section white and the tail blue. I helped him secure the wire hooks on the top so it could be raced on a thicker metal wire stretched across the gymnasium during the next Den meeting.

My wife took him to the meeting while I bowled on Tuesday nights. I made it back to the school in time to watch the elimination rounds. The leaders used a drill to wind up the rubber band 100 times or so. Then the Boy Scouts carefully placed their rockets on the metal wires and launched them on cue. The propeller released all that kinetic energy and two brightly colored rockets went careening across the school gym with a trail of uniformed boys screeching behind them.

During the first flight, Steve's rocket was half way across the gymnasium before anyone else's rocket passed the quarter mark. The leaders couldn't understand why it was so fast. They inspected and reinspected his rocket to see if we had altered the design somehow. They kept asking us what we did to the rocket. We didn't do anything.

It took a retired Air Force flight engineer to figure it out. There were two small wire hooks that we pushed into the wood on the top that allowed us to hang the rocket on the wire. I later discovered that our front wire was a little bit higher than the back wire. Consequently the nose was up. So, when we raced the rocket, it pulled the nose up. There was less drag on it. That's the only thing I could figure.

Bob's Cub Scout troop held a pine box racing derby. He was given a piece of wood about six inches long and some wheels. His instructions were to build out the race car, but ensure that it didn't weigh more than five ounces. We worked on it at home, putting BB pellets in the wheels and painting it together. We made a regular race car out of it. Before the next meeting, I weighed the car on one of the post office's scales.

Again, I was bowling with my team on Tuesday night when Bob was at Scouts. When I arrived the boys were still racing and cheering each other on. Bob had won his earlier rounds and was setting up for the championship match. When the cars got to the bottom of the track, Bob's car was leading by half a length. The other boy's car suddenly jumped over the rail and bumped Bob's car off the tracks. We argued unsuccessfully for a disqualification.

My wife and I had some pretty good times with the boys. She enjoyed being a Boy Scout mother.

All these years later I've kept Bob's trophy from the Kite Flying Contest in the Indian Guides, because it was the most important trophy I had in my house. It was Bob's trophy. It meant something to him. Over the years I've had other trophies, bowling trophies and such, that I won myself. None of them meant as much to me as any trophy won by my sons.

My wife and I weren't homebodies. We always had fun going out and discovering new things. We liked to get in the car and travel. There was no formal plan to continuously discover new vacation spots, but that's what we did. We wanted the boys to experience life, to see different places and have the opportunity to learn. We went up and down the East Coast with them. My wife would find a place she'd like to take them to visit and we'd try to make it happen.

When Jim was a baby we went tent camping with friends. It was a lot of fun camping with a group of people, pitching tents together and cooking around a camp fire. Eventually we took all the boys camping.

The family road trips included Santa's Workshop at Santa Land in Denville, New Jersey; Disney World the year it opened in 1971, Wild West City in Netcong, New Jersey; Fort Ticonderoga in New York; Washington DC where we saw the Washington Monument and got to shoot guns downstairs in the FBI building; Virginia; ski trips; dozens of trips to the New Jersey shore with my sister in law, Margaret's family; and an infinite number of fishing trips. We made every effort possible to take the boys to places they wanted to go.

At Fort Ticonderoga, I remember Jim being one of the first children to volunteer during a stage coach run. Being the oldest, he was always the most forward. He never stood back. The staff picked three children to go up on stage and Jim was the first one picked to ride the stage coach. They needed little guards to protect the stage coach during the show. He jumped right into the task. At the same time Steve got picked to be a soldier. I'll never forget how the captain's raspy boom of a voice frightened all the little recruits. Steve pushed right up against the next guy.

Fishing is a four-season sport for us. We can still be ready to go in just a few minutes and when we're not fishing we are either talking about our last trip or planning the next one. One cold winter, Bob asked if he could go fishing with a friend in about ten days at Vernon Valley, a ski resort area about fifty miles from Summit in northwestern Sussex County. We said sure. The night before we left a wall of snow fell over the northern part of the state and the roads were fairly impassable. My wife decided to stay back home and we gave the trip a try, but I told Bob if the roads became worse then we were turning around. Well, we got there and we fished. The boys were thankful when we came home. Sometimes we did things for the boys that were a little difficult for us. Their appreciation and joy over having made the trip, however, made the effort worth it.

As a family we had a lot of fishing experience that all began in Chatham. My sons and I fished there growing up. Each spring the fire department stocked the local pond with trout and hosted its annual fishing derby. My sons participated in the derby when they were young. It was even more rewarding the year my granddaughters, Felica and Monica, joined me. Felica was about 14 years old. I bought them both fishing poles. Darn, if they didn't catch the two biggest fish that day. Because they were not residents they weren't supposed to win. The event director called me later that day, however, and said the girls won two fishing tackle boxes. They enjoyed it very much. For me, it was fun to pass on a family tradition to the next generation.

When we took Jim to college in North Carolina we planned a side-trip vacation to Nags Head for a few days. Bob, who was in middle school at the time, wanted to fish. We found a pier for the morning. Bob set up next to an elderly gentleman and watched him reel fish after fish up the line. Finally, Bob asked him what he was using for bait. The man bent over his bucket, dug in and showed him a handful of small soft shell crabs, offering up a sample. Bob threw out his line with two hooks on it and, sure enough, brought up two decent size fish. We snapped a victory photo of him with his fresh catch.

Sometimes on the weekends Virginia just liked to go for a car ride. Since I wasn't working most weekends, we often drove all around northern New Jersey. She loved it most in the fall when the trees throughout the Highlands region put on their own art show with strokes of red, orange, yellow and green. Sometimes we went shopping and sometimes we just wanted to look around and then stop to eat.

When we were first married and working, Virginia and I had a lot of fun going out with other couples. After the children were born we were lucky in that we still got to keep our date night. We had a good baby sitter in my mother in law. Our date spot was Marco Polo, a gem of a restaurant on Morris Avenue in Summit where a pretty good crowd came to hear a band play on the second floor every Saturday night. My wife liked that a lot. She got to know the musicians well.

Whenever they saw her they always played her favorite songs, including a lot of Tony Bennett's music.

We took four big trips in our marriage. For our 25th wedding anniversary I talked Virginia into going on a cruise to Bermuda with two other couples. We had such a good time on that trip that we took three other cruises, including one to Alaska and another to Aruba. The majestic shorelines and constant awe-inspiring vistas of Alaska were our favorites. That's what we did when I retired.

My Virginia passed away in 2000, just before our 50th wedding anniversary. I can still see her in every room of our house. This was our dream - our American dream - and it is the final and most important story of my military history. It is the life we've lived.

Gerard Caporaso at Bushkill Falls in
Pennsylvania in the late 1940's.

MY VIRGINIA

Virginia (Stanek) Caporaso at Bushkill Falls in Pennsylvania in the late 1940's while she was dating Gerard Caporaso.

FROM THE TOP TURRET

Virginia and Gerard Caporaso standing on the back of a
Chatham Fire Department truck on their wedding day, Sept. 1, 1951.

MY VIRGINIA

Family portrait of Virginia and Gerard Caporaso's sons, Robert, Steven, and James. 1962.

Caporaso Family portrait - (Back row) Steven, Gerard, James and Robert Caporaso. (Front row) Felicia, Mary, Monica, Kate, Maureen, and Elizabeth Caporaso. 2001

Virginia and Gerard Caporaso on a cruise ship.

Caporaso family picnic in 2000. Virginia and Gerard Caporaso are sitting under the umbrella.

The Caporaso family home in Summit, New Jersey. August 2012.

Gerard Caporaso at Chatham Fire Department. May 2012.

Chatham Fire Department, 1976.

Chatham, New Jersey Post Office. May 2012.

Chatham Veterans Memorial, Route 24, Chatham, N.J. May 2012.

Chapter 13

LOOKING BACK

They said the life of a gunner is 20 or 30 seconds long. I was just a wide-eyed kid when I heard that statement in 1942. How quickly I learned the truth that in war every second of life is precious.

More than 70 years later I am still hanging on to my 30 seconds, enjoying each day, living for those who couldn't and making sure our enemy didn't win. I would not let the tragic events of my youth define my entire life.

I'll tell you one thing, however. Having survived World War II made me realize that the United States of America is my country. I traveled to a number of countries abroad during the war and there is no comparison. We do a lot for other countries around the world and they don't necessarily appreciate it. Having served in the military helped me to understand the United States. It made me proud to be home. We have a good country here. If we ever had another war where I had to defend our country I would be there again if I could. Home is worth fighting for.

Once I came home from the war, I returned to civilian life, started a career, married my dear wife Virginia and raised three sons. I have survived bad knees, heart trouble, dietary issues and cancer. I've been blessed with two daughter in-laws, Maureen and Mary, who gave me four beautiful granddaughters, Felica,

FROM THE TOP TURRET

Monica, Elizabeth and Kathleen, I adore. I am surrounded by nieces, nephews and friends.

This life I've cherished. I am still buzzing Chatham.

Love
Jerry

Chapter 14

REFLECTIONS FROM MY SONS

Jim Caporaso

My father is one of the sweetest men you will ever meet. When I was a kid I can remember going along with him to the firehouse and Dad's softball games. I loved to hang out with him.

We would drive to Chatham on Saturdays to get our crew cuts. I remember, when he would hug me, the rough feeling of his beard scraping the soft skin of my face and the smell of Old Spice aftershave.

One time the fire alarm went off while we were getting our crew cuts and we ran the two blocks together to the firehouse. I was about eight or nine years old. Alarms were sounding and it was a real emergency. Like any small boy at the moment, I was both excited and terrified at the rush of action. I watched Dad and the other men race to grab all their fire fighting gear, check equipment and move three giant engines out of the building. I even had a chance to ride to the fire in the firetruck with them, but I was too scared. As they pulled away with great urgency, I stayed behind at the fire house and just waited for Dad. I learned a lot from my father's volunteer fire department service, his service to our country in World War II and his survival as a prisoner of war. I grew up always grateful for men like him, who sacrificed so much so that I never had to go to war myself.

The best word to describe Dad is solid. I knew he was always there for us. Even in his nineties, he still is. We did not have a lot growing up, in terms of fancy cars or fancy clothes, but we had everything we needed. Everything that mattered. We always had vacations, many times staying with relatives in North Carolina or Florida. Even on a budget, we managed to see the New Jersey shore, beaches in North Carolina and Florida, Disney World, Washington, DC and a memorable trip camping in a cabin in Maine. A love for the outdoors was instilled in us early and I still have that with me. I will always remember fishing as something important we shared. Even now, just before his 91st birthday, my brothers and I managed to get a fishing trip in together with Dad, who can still reel them in from a wheelchair.

I did not understand the depth of my father's love for my mother, his wife Ginny, until she passed away. Only then did it become clear how much they loved each other and how he truly lost the love of his live. For a few weeks after her passing Dad had a hard time accepting that she was gone. He still misses her to this day. They sacrificed a lot for my brothers and I, so much that it's easy to forget how they fell in love and had an amazing life together before we were born. They were partners. When we did arrive, they became great parents, who raised us in a great hometown in Summit, New Jersey. They supported us all to graduate from college and go on to live successful happy lives.

I feel very lucky to still have my Dad with me at 55 years of age and still in Summit. I love him very much and miss him since I live in North Carolina. I am so grateful for my brothers, who have been there for him. The author Thomas Wolfe was wrong. You can go home again if your Dad is still alive and he loves you.

Steve Caporaso

Looking back over my father's life the one thing that stands out that I'd like to remember is what a hard worker he was. I was always amazed.

One of the things I did with him on a regular basis was getting up extra early in the morning, before everyone else woke up. We both live by the philosophy of early to bed, early to rise. That's how he lived and that's how I live. When Dad was a supervisor at the Chatham Post Office before he became an assistant post master and had regular hours, he went into work at 5 o'clock in the morning. When I was a young kid the television only had channels two through thirteen. Stations still signed off at night. At five a.m. there was only one channel on and it was the farm channel. I used to hide from my father as I sneaked downstairs to watch the farming programs in black and white on a 13-inch television in the family room. He knew I was down there. He'd be talking to himself saying, "I'm going to work," while he was trying to find me. Eventually he did. We did that a lot. It was part of our early morning routine.

I always admired how hard he worked. He had a job where he didn't make a ton of money, but he showed up for the job every single day and worked hard all day without complaint and then came home to us. That's a work ethic that set a huge example for my brothers and me.

My father and mother gave us the best childhood they could. Their biggest goal was to be able to send their three sons to college. They had friends who had more means and, yet, their children didn't make it to college. We were a typical middle-class family. My Mom worked before we were born and, when we were a little older and more self sufficient, she went back to work to help put us through college. I'm convinced that she went back to work in order to make that happen and my parents both worked as hard as they could to realize that dream together.

I am so grateful to them for making that possible for us. I wasn't the greatest college student in the world. I struggled my first year and had to take an extended stay in college. They kept me on track and supported me. They wanted to see me get through to graduation and I did. We all did. It was just so important to my parents that we all got college degrees and they worked their lives for that. My mother may not have wanted to go back to work and my father was going to work as hard as he did whether we were going to college or not. I've always admired his work ethic and that's something I've tried to mimic.

By way of example, when my Dad was still working he hurt his knee and needed to take some time off. He wasn't comfortable with taking sick days. In his mind that equated to time for himself and that just wasn't in his genetic makeup. Yet, he already had a year and half of vacation time saved up at work, because he never took time off. Not only did he get his health leave to have his knee repaired, but he also got his vacation time.

When I think about the example my father set for me I look back on how hard I've worked in my own career. In the last 20 years I've probably taken four sick days. Once you get into work you work. That's how Dad was.

That same work ethic held true with Dad's work in the Chatham Fire Department. When he was at the department it was the most important thing to him. That was all volunteer time and every job he held was the most important job in the world to get done correctly. Every fire was the most important fire, because it was a crisis to someone in town and he was dedicated to help them through it.

For more than 30 years Dad managed the annual Fourth of July parade in Chatham. It was always a highlight in our lives going to the parade and feeling like we were the to-do kids going to the fireworks. As kids we pumped out our chests a little bit, because we were proud of the fact that Dad did it every year and it was something we greatly enjoyed. The parade was a big deal and it was a big part of our lives.

The year after my father gave up the role as parade chairman he was honored as the grand marshal. I have a beautiful photo of my Dad riding in the back seat of a convertible in the parade with my two daughters in the car. It was such a rewarding way to end his role in that event.

Until about 15 years ago my Dad still managed the administrative end of the fire department, helping members with health and death benefits. He was fearful to give up the job to another member, who may not take as much care with it as he did. Dad is still a department member and still attends the monthly meetings, even though he doesn't fight fires anymore. It's still his boys club. It's still where he likes to go. He's far older now, but the other members respect him and still like to have him over.

As we got older the fire department began hosting an annual golf outing. In the early days we would play as a family and my father played with us. I think we won the tournament twice. Until about six years ago we were still a foursome that had the potential to win. Dad is competitive. When he goes with us, even when he's just riding alongside us in a cart, he's still expecting us to win it for him. I always tell him that we'll win it for him again: maybe.

The fire department was such a big part of his life and I've always respected him for it. Knowing the depth of my father's work with the department, I hold the highest regard for anyone who volunteers their time and puts their life at risk for others.

There are several family memories that my parents gave to us that linger like they happened just a few years ago. My father talked about a few of them. I'd like to elaborate on those stories from my own perspective.

Grandparents

My father talked about family dinners and how the entire extended family got together for Sunday and holiday dinners. I can remember going to our grandparents house on Butler Parkway in Summit after church on Sundays to eat lunch. My grandmother was an extremely talented cook and knew how to feed a hungry crowd. As kids we'd eat so much spaghetti and meatballs that all we could do was crawl to the couch and pass out for a few hours until we digested what we ate.

Games in the yard

Being the corner lot and the biggest lot in the neighborhood, our backyard truly was the second playground in Summit. The rules were always changing, because as we grew the games became bigger or rougher. My friends and I played endless hours of Wiffle Ball on the side yard and hit it off the backyard fence. As we got bigger, however, we were wrapping baseballs off the side of the house and breaking shingles off the house. My father would scold us saying, "You can't be breaking shingles off the house." So we adjusted the rules of the games so that if you hit the house you were automatically out. Bases had to be moved, because we were wearing out grass. Games were always changing to accommodate different things around the house. My parents were happy to see all the kids playing in the yard, even though the yard and the house took a beating occasionally.

On the Little League strike out

My father was the umpire that all umpires went to for questions. He was rule master. Whenever there was a question on games my father could say, "Yes, that's rule number 13-32A on page twelve of the rule book and open up the book to it. He was without a doubt the most respected umpire in the game. That's how he got to be named home umpire behind the plate for the Summit All-Star Championship game I was playing. Fathers didn't typically umpire their sons games. Dad officiated as many games as he could and managed my team with coach Don Reiger.

Dad tells his story and I tell mine. We'll debate it until the end of time. I didn't think that last pitch was a perfect pitch. It was outside and high. Dad struck me out. I certainly didn't argue, but I completely disagreed with his call. Knowing my father the way he was, he wasn't going to let anyone think he gave me a break. I don't think in his mind he gave me a break. He called balls and strikes. He thought it was a strike and I thought it was a ball. We'll disagree forever. I vaguely remember the parents questioning him.

The Boy Scout rocket race

The funny part about my Dad's telling the story about my rocket race in Boy Scouts was the turn of events it created for me. When our scout troop held the Pinewood Derby every year with little wooden cars my car always crashed. I always lost and left depressed. One year no one wanted to race against me, because they feared that my car was going to jump the tracks and knock them out of the race. That only added to the excitement of the rocket race that followed the next year.

The rockets came pre-made. All I had to do was paint it and put the two hooks in the top so that it could race along a wire. My father was right in that one hook was hire than another. My rocket beat everyone by half the length of the gym in every race. Every parent in the facility was looking at my rocket all night long for something we did, assuming we were cheating one way or another. It took an aviation engineer to figure it out. The front hook, being higher, caused the rocket to lift.

The Cowbell

Mom had an old fashioned metal cowbell on the window sill in the kitchen that she used to call us kids home to dinner. Everyone in the neighborhood had some kind of bell, because we kids were always outside playing. At our soccer games Mom always had the bell with her to cheer us on and Dad could always find us. Like everything they did together for us, my parents worked hard and found a way to keep cheering us on. Still.

Bob Caporaso

There's something to be said about the life lessons learned by a great example set for you quietly and diligently every day over a long and fulfilled life. That's the gift my Dad gave us.

He didn't seek accolades for all the hard work he did. He did what he was supposed to do every single day of his life and made sure he was present with us for everything we did in our childhood. Yet, he still managed to find time to commit himself to the fire department for more than sixty seven years, making sure he was also available to help the residents of Chatham, New Jersey. That strength and reliability still exists today.

When I think back to how my father influenced my life three things stand out: presence, education and foundation. He was the greatest of mentors.

While I was growing up he was always there for everything we were doing, whether it was for myself, Steve or Jim. For me especially, whether it was Indian Guides or going camping, he was always involved in everything I did. He guided us, encouraged us, and made it fun.

Once in the middle of the winter we went ice fishing in Cub Scouts and none of the other boys wanted to go out into the middle of the frozen lake. Dad knew I loved to fish. Looking back on it now, I knew I wasn't going to catch anything.

Still he took me out into the middle of the lake in the dead of winter at 6 o'clock at night. It was pitch black. He dragged a manual auger with him after work and drilled through two feet of ice. He did it for me, because he knew how much it meant to me. It was the same thing with Cub Scouts' pinewood derby or the rocket races. He was just always there and made that commitment. He did it for us. That dedication in responsibility resonates with my brothers and me today

When we got into sports, whether it was team sports or individual sports, he was just always there and he wanted to participate. Looking back, I know I acted like a classic teenager whose father was always involved and around. Still, he showed up. I know many people can say that about their parents, too, but I also know many who can't say that was true in their home. Today I can look back and really appreciate the effort my father made to spend time with us, even though at the time I certainly didn't express it.

When I was in Little League he was always there at my games, even when he was off umpiring. He'd finish his games and come back to watch mine or Jim and Steve's. Even individual sports had a priority in our house. The opening day of trout fishing season in New Jersey was a family outing that required us to get up before dawn, load up the car together and drive to the Musconetcong River. It was an annual adventure that had us waist-deep in ice cold spring waters in New Jersey, standing side by side in waders, and ended with a hearty breakfast at the Chester Diner.

A couple of the fishing trips we took with Dad as kids still stand out in our collective memories. Once in Florida we took a fishing trip on the St. John River, a well known bass fishing river similar to the Everglades. It was an entire day of just hanging out and fishing large.

On our vacation to Disney World in 1971 we went fishing for hours on these brackish lakes in the blaring hot Florida sun and burnt to a crisp. Steve ended up hooking a monstrous red drum, probably a 25-pounder, and then couldn't hold it. The fish outmuscled him. Being a little brother, I ribbed him for it at the time. To this day I still do. We were so sunburned from the long day, however, that we cried all night. We didn't care, because we got to go fishing.

Another time we were fishing in Florida with a family friend we called Uncle Chuck, a retired Marine who didn't use very good judgment, when a hurricane blew up the coast. The use of Doppler radar in weather forecasting wasn't as commonplace in 1971 as it is today. We were in Uncle Chuck's camper on the beach, behind the dunes, anchored down with four old telephone poles when the hurricane rocked that silver bullet camper with 70 to 80 mile per hour winds. Fishing ended early and we got stuck there for the night. Steve, who was probably eight years old, opened the door to the camper and got sucked out by the wind and thrown down the dunes. It was funny at the time watching Dad and Uncle Chuck tearing off after him. But we were fishing.

Dad made a big deal about the events in our lives that were important to us. He was always committed to us, always encouraging us to get out there and do our best. He probably enjoyed the commotion more than we did sometimes.

Providing us with a strong education was my parents' life goal. They wanted to raise us in a good public school system and do whatever it took to provide us with a college education.

Jim went to the University of North Carolina and Steve went to West Virginia University, both of which were costly schools. Putting two kids through college was enough of a sacrifice for my parents, let alone three. When I started looking at colleges I wanted to attend Northeastern University for its information technology program, which was twice as expensive as my brothers' schools. I sat down with my parents and discussed all the reasons why I felt I needed to be there. Before I left for my first year my Dad and I had a long talk. He said he just wanted to set us up to be successful by establishing the foundation that we built the rest of our lives on. In an era of student loans, when everyone was getting their hands on cheap money, he and my mother still wanted us to come out of school without a mountain of debt. They made it happen. Only in the last ten years did my Dad tell me that he and my Mom were living paycheck to paycheck for a few years. I was so surprised. That strengthened my admiration for my parent's commitment and the lengths they went to make this a reality.

I deeply appreciate everything they did for me. Were it not for my parents' sacrifice I wouldn't be where I am today. I specifically went to Northeastern to get into the high tech industry. In the 1980s, Boston and Silicon Valley were the places to be and I needed to get there through the university's co-op program. I've been fortunate to have a successful and exciting career in IT. My parents recognize that.

My parents have always been there and always tried to contribute in helping us grow. They are a great strength in my life. Looking back, I feel such gratitude and love for the lessons they gave me. Yet, the journey was filled with stories that my brothers and I are still retelling and laughing about.

FROM THE TOP TURRET

Gerard and Robert Caporaso under the bomb bay of a restored B-17 on tour with the Collings Foundation at Monmouth Executive Airport, Wall, N.J. in September 2011.

Gerard Caporaso standing under the bomb bay of a restored B-17 on tour with the Collings Foundation at Monmouth Executive Airport, Wall, N.J. in September 2011.

Gerard Caporaso under the wing of a restored B-17 on tour with the Collings Foundation at Monmouth Executive Airport, Wall, N.J. in September 2011.

FROM THE TOP TURRET

Robert Caporaso, Gerard Caporaso, Brigid O'Donnell and Steven Caporaso during a reunion with O'Donnell at Gerard's home in Summit, N.J. on November 5, 2012.

REFLECTIONS FROM MY SONS

(Left) Gerard Caporaso holding some of his military patches and pins. (Below) Gerard Caporaso's dog tags, P-38, and U.S. Army Air Force pins.

FROM THE TOP TURRET

U.S. Army Air Force flight jacket with dog tags, pins, P-38, sergeant stripes and Eighth Air Force patch.

REFLECTIONS FROM MY SONS

Gerard Caporaso holding his U.S. Army Air Force
flight jacket with dog tags and pins.

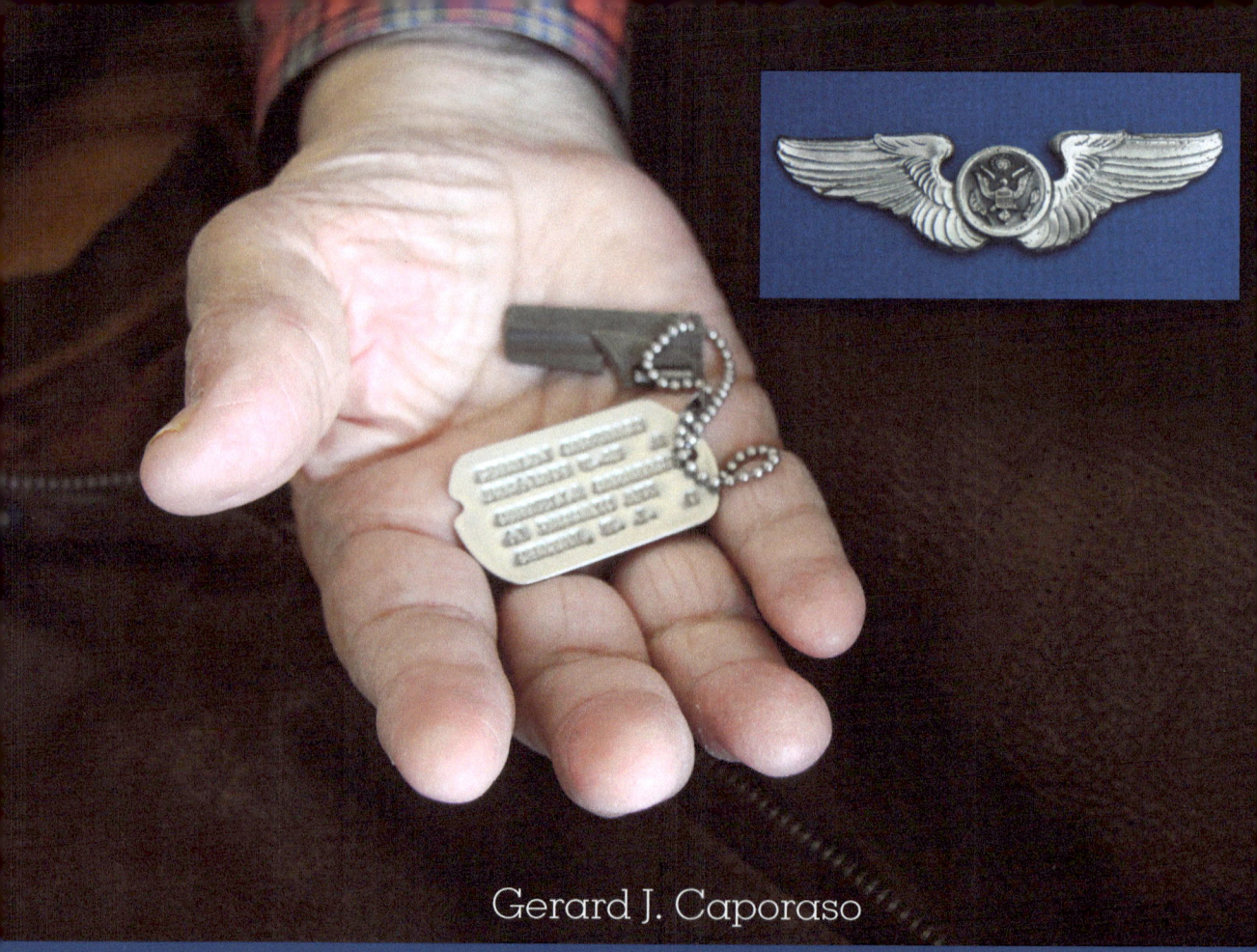

Gerard J. Caporaso

Master Sergeant Retired • US Eighth Air Force • Third Air Division
45th Combat Wing • 337th Bomb Squadron • 96th Bomb Group
Top Turret Gunner • Flight Maintenance Gunner 748

Decorations & Citations

Distinguished Service Medal
Air Medal
Prisoner of War Medal
World War II Victory Medal
European African Middle Eastern Campaign Medal with 1 Bronze Star
American Campaign Medal
Good Conduct Medal
Dog Tags (USAAF, Stalag XVIIB)
Army Air Force Tech Badge with AP Mechanic Gunner Bar
3 Overseas bars
US Eighth Air Force patch
Lapel pin

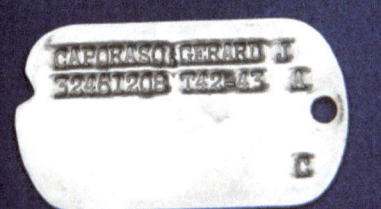

Army of the United States

Honorable Discharge

This is to certify that

GERARD J CAPORASO 32 461 208 Master Sergeant

337th Bomb Squadron
96th Bomb Group

Army of the United States

is hereby Honorably Discharged from the military service of the United States of America.

This certificate is awarded as a testimonial of Honest and Faithful Service to this country.

Given at Separation Base
Rome AAFld Rome New York

Date 7 November 1945

WILLIAM L CHIPMAN
Major AC

Received & Recorded Nov 23 1945
In Book A-1 of "Honorable Discharges of Veterans" on Page 531&c
E. BERTRAM MOTT, Clerk

ENLISTED RECORD AND REPORT OF SEPARATION
HONORABLE DISCHARGE

1. LAST NAME - FIRST NAME - MIDDLE INITIAL	2. ARMY SERIAL NO.	3. GRADE	4. ARM OR SERVICE	5. COMPONENT
CAPORASO GERARD J	32 461 208	M/Sgt	AC	AUS

6. ORGANIZATION	7. DATE OF SEPARATION	8. PLACE OF SEPARATION
337th Bomb Squadron 96th Bomb Group	7 November 45	Separation Base RAAFld New York

9. PERMANENT ADDRESS FOR MAILING PURPOSES	10. DATE OF BIRTH	11. PLACE OF BIRTH
61 Passaic Ave Chatham New Jersey	15 June 1921	Chatham New Jersey

12. ADDRESS FROM WHICH EMPLOYMENT WILL BE SOUGHT	13. COLOR EYES	14. COLOR HAIR	15. HEIGHT	16. WEIGHT	17. NO. DEPEND.
See 9	Brown	Brown	5'6 1/4"	148 LBS.	0

18. RACE	19. MARITAL STATUS	20. U.S. CITIZEN	21. CIVILIAN OCCUPATION AND NO.
WHITE X NEGRO OTHER	SINGLE X MARRIED OTHER	YES X NO	Stock Clerk 1-38.01

MILITARY HISTORY

22. DATE OF INDUCTION	23. DATE OF ENLISTMENT	24. DATE OF ENTRY INTO ACTIVE SERVICE	25. PLACE OF ENTRY INTO SERVICE
19 August 42		2 Sept 1942	Fort Dix New Jersey

SELECTIVE SERVICE DATA	26. REGISTERED	27. LOCAL S.S. BOARD NO.	28. COUNTY AND STATE	29. HOME ADDRESS AT TIME OF ENTRY INTO SERVICE
	YES X NO	1	Morris Co New Jersey	61 Passaic Ave Chatham New Jersey

30. MILITARY OCCUPATIONAL SPECIALTY AND NO.	31. MILITARY QUALIFICATION AND DATE
Flight Maintenance Gunner 748	AAF Tech Badge with Ap Mech Gunr Bar

32. BATTLES AND CAMPAIGNS
Air Offensive Europe

33. DECORATIONS AND CITATIONS
Air Medal   3 Overseas Bars   World War II Victory Medal   Good Conduct Medal
American Campaign Medal   European African Middle Eastern Campaign Medal with 1 Bronze Star.

34. WOUNDS RECEIVED IN ACTION
None

35. LATEST IMMUNIZATION DATES

SMALLPOX	TYPHOID	TETANUS	OTHER (specify)
17 Jul 43	8 Aug 43	17 Nov 43	See 55

36. SERVICE OUTSIDE CONTINENTAL U.S. AND RETURN

DATE OF DEPARTURE	DESTINATION	DATE OF ARRIVAL
22 Aug 43	ETO	31 Aug 43
1 June 45	USA	12 June 45

37. TOTAL LENGTH OF SERVICE

CONTINENTAL SERVICE			FOREIGN SERVICE			38. HIGHEST GRADE HELD
YEARS	MONTHS	DAYS	YEARS	MONTHS	DAYS	
1	3	15	1	10	20	M/Sgt

39. PRIOR SERVICE
None

40. REASON AND AUTHORITY FOR SEPARATION
Convn of Govt AR 615-365 RR 1-1 Demobilization 15 Dec 44

41. SERVICE SCHOOLS ATTENDED Amarillo Texas Ap & Engine Mech 14 wks Seattle Wash
Ap & Eng B-17 4 wks Las Vegas Nev Air Gunner 5 wks

42. EDUCATION (Years)		
Grammar	High School	College
8	4	0

PAY DATA

43. LONGEVITY FOR PAY PURPOSES			44. MUSTERING OUT PAY		45. SOLDIER DEPOSITS	46. TRAVEL PAY	47. TOTAL AMOUNT, NAME OF DISBURSING OFFICER
YEARS	MONTHS	DAYS	TOTAL	THIS PAYMENT			
3	2	18	$300.	$100.	0	$12.55	$146.36 PERCY W NEWTON Maj AC

INSURANCE NOTICE

IMPORTANT: IF PREMIUM IS NOT PAID WHEN DUE OR WITHIN THIRTY-ONE DAYS THEREAFTER, INSURANCE WILL LAPSE. MAKE CHECKS OR MONEY ORDERS PAYABLE TO THE TREASURER OF THE U.S. AND FORWARD TO COLLECTIONS SUBDIVISION, VETERANS ADMINISTRATION, WASHINGTON 25, D.C.

48. KIND OF INSURANCE	49. HOW PAID	50. Effective Date of Allotment Discontinuance	51. Date of Next Premium Due (One month after 50)	52. PREMIUM DUE EACH MONTH	53. INTENTION OF VETERAN TO
Nat. Serv. X U.S. Govt. None	Allotment X Direct to V.A.	31 Oct 45	30 Nov 45	$6.55	Continue Continue Only Discontinue

55. REMARKS
Add Immunization Dates-   Lapel Button Issued
Yellow Fever-1 June 43
Typhus-21 May 45
Cholera-30 Apr 43

ASR Score (2 Sept 45) 67

APPLICATION FOR READJUSTMENT ALLOWANCES MADE THROUGH THE UNEMPLOYMENT COMPENSATION COMMISSION OF NEW JERSEY
ON 1-9-46

56. SIGNATURE OF PERSON BEING SEPARATED
Gerard J. Caporaso

57. PERSONNEL OFFICER
D A PETERSON
Capt AC

WD AGO FORM 53-55
1 November 1944

REFLECTIONS FROM MY SONS

(Opposite page) Gerard Caporaso sitting in his living room holding his U.S. Army Air Force medals and citations with World War II memorabilia on the table. August 2012. (Above) Gerard Caporaso sitting inside a B-17 bomber on tour with the Collings Foundation at Morristown Airport, Morristown, New Jersey. August 2012. (Bottom) Plane on takeoff.

FROM THE TOP TURRET

(Above) View looking up the top turret inside a B-17 bomber. (Left) View of the nose gunner post inside a B-17 bomber flying over Morris County, New Jersey.

View of the top turret, taken from the center of the plane in flight looking forward.

View of a B-17 bomber tail section in flight, taken from the center of the plane looking backward.

View of a B-17 bomber on takeoff from Morristown Airport, Morristown, New Jersey in August 2012. One of Gerard Caporaso's wishes was to fly again in a restored B-17. On August 24, 2012, a perfectly clear summer day, he went on a hour-long flight over Morris County, New Jersey with his sons, Steven and Robert, and co-author Mary Danielsen. Ironically, the day before the flight the B-17 flew over his home in Summit, buzzing him once again. Photo reprinted with permission by Charles Salin.

PHOTOGRAPHY CAPTIONS & CREDITS

Front Cover Photo Photo: Mary V. Danielsen

Back Cover Photo U.S. Army Air Force photo of Gerard J. Caporaso in flight suit. Caporaso family photos

Inside Title Page: Top turret. Photo: Mary V. Danielsen

Prologue: Photo of Gerard Caporaso with granddaughters. (From left) Monica, Felicia, Gerard, Beth and Kate Caporaso, 2001. Caporaso family photos

First insert - Early Chatham Photos
(After Chapter 2)
Boy Scout Troop photo - Gerard Caporaso is in the back row, third from the right. Caporaso Family Photos

Downtown Chatham Postcard, 1930's. Caporaso family archives

Photo of Carmela Caporaso, mother of Gerard J. Caporaso. Caporaso family archives

Photo of Carmine "Frank" Caporaso, father of Gerard J. Caporaso. Caporaso family archives

Second insert - Early Air Force & Crew Photos
(After Chapter 4)
Official portrait Gerard J. Caporaso, U.S. Army Air Force 1942. Caporaso family photos

Photo of military gear on cots outside barracks at Amarillo Field, Amarillo, Texas. Nov. 9, 1942. Caporaso family archives

Photo of new barracks and dirt pathways at Amarillo Field, Amarillo, Texas Nov. 9, 1942 Caporaso family archives

Photo of Gerard Caporaso and Mrs. F. Polter and her daughter Gail in Amarillo, Texas. Mrs. Polter hosted several Air Force soldiers for Thanksgiving dinner. November 1942. Caporaso family archives.

Photo of Gerard Caporaso in uniform outside barracks at Amarillo Field, Amarillo, Texas. 1942. Caporaso family archives

Photo of Gerard Caporaso on horseback on top of a mountain in Palo Duro Canyon State Park, Texas. January 4, 1943. Caporaso family archives

Photo of Gerard Caporaso with (from left) Warren Caldwell of Maiden, North Carolina, E. Carnivale of New York, and Denis Carey of New York in Palo Duro Canyon State Park, Texas They discovered a wild hog while riding horseback in the canyon. January 4, 1943. Caporaso family archives

Photo of (from left) Victor Carozzo of Delaware, Gerard Caporaso and Warren Caldwell of Maiden, North Carolina on furlough in El Paso, Texas on April 21, 1943.

Photo of Gerard Caporaso with E. Carnivale, McIntyre, Warren Caldwell of Maiden, North Carolina and Burrows at the Boeing facility in Seattle, Washington where they were sent for training on B-17 bombers on Feb 7, 1943. Caporaso family archives

Photo of Gerard J. Caporaso on base. Photo: Lt. Raymond F. Bye. Photo provided from the private collection of Brigid Bye O'Donnell and reproduced with permission of Brigid Bye O'Donnell.

PHOTOGRAPHY CAPTIONS & CREDITS

Photo of Crew K90 in Iceland, August 1943. Gerard Caporaso is second from the right, standing in back row. Photo: Lt. Raymond F. Bye. Photo provided from the private collection of Brigid Bye O'Donnell and reproduced with permission of Brigid Bye O'Donnell.

Official portrait Lt. Raymond F. Bye, U.S. Army Air Force, 1942. Photo provided from the private collection of Brigid Bye O'Donnell and reproduced with permission of Brigid Bye O'Donnell.

Crew K90 group photo, signed by crew members and identified below. Photo: Lt. Raymond F. Bye. Photo provided from the private collection of Brigid Bye O'Donnell and reproduced with permission of Brigid Bye O'Donnell.

Photo of a B-17 in flight during World War II. Caporaso family photos

Third Insert - Serving in the War
(After Chapter 7)
Photo of Snetterton Heath Air Force base, UK, Feb. 1946. Photo: National Archives

Photo of B-17 bomber, Dottie J III, crashed in farm field outside Thiaucourt, France, showing plane from left side. German officer and tent under the wing. Photo provided from the private collection of Brigid Bye O'Donnell and reproduced with permission of Brigid Bye O'Donnell.

Photo of B-17 bomber, Dottie J III, crashed in farm field outside Thiaucourt, France, showing plane from right side. German officer standing in the back behind burned out engine. Photo provided from the private collection of Brigid Bye O'Donnell and reproduced with permission of Brigid Bye O'Donnell.

Ariel photo of Stalag XVIIB outside Krems, Austria. Photo: National Archives

Photo of Certificate of Merit earned by Gerard Caporaso at the Interned Airmen's Institute at Stalag XVIIB. Caporaso family archives

Final letter home from war, dated May 17, 1945, telling Gerard's mother that he will be home soon. Caporaso family archives

Photo of Gerard Caporaso after receiving his Honorable Discharge from military service in Syracuse, New York on Nov. 16, 1945. Caporaso family archives

Fourth insert - Family Photos
(After Chapter 12)
Photo of Gerard Caporaso at Bushkill Falls in Pennsylvania in the late 1940's. Caporaso family archives

Photo of Virginia (Stanek) Caporaso at Bushkill Falls in Pennsylvania in the late 1940's while she and Gerard Caporaso were dating. Caporaso family archives

Wedding photo of Virginia and Gerard Caporaso, Sept. 1, 1951. Caporaso family photos

Portrait of Robert, Steven and James Caporaso, 1962. Caporaso family photos

Portrait of Caporaso Family in 2001. (Back row) Steven, Gerard, James and Robert Caporaso. (Front row) Felicia, Mary, Monica, Kate, Maureen, and Elizabeth Caporaso. Caporaso family photo

Photo Virginia and Gerard Caporaso on cruise ship. Caporaso family photos

Photo Caporaso family picnic, 2000. Virginia and Gerard Caporaso are sitting under the umbrella. Caporaso family photos

Photo of Caporaso family home, August 2012. Photo: Mary V. Danielsen

Portrait of Gerard Caporaso in Chatham Fire Department uniform at the firehouse, May 2012. Photo: Mary V. Danielsen

Antique postcard of Chatham Fire Department, 1976. Caporaso family archives

Photo of front of Chatham, New Jersey Post Office, May 2012. Photo: Mary V. Danielsen

Photo of Chatham Veterans Memorial, Route 24, Chatham, N.J. May 2012. Photo: Mary V. Danielsen

PHOTOGRAPHY CAPTIONS & CREDITS

Fifth Insert - Looking Back
(After Chapter 14)
Photo of Gerard and Robert Caporaso under the bomb bay of a restored B-17 on tour with the Collings Foundation of Stow, Mass at Monmouth Executive Airport, Wall, NJ Sept. 2011. Photo: Mary V. Danielsen

Photo of Gerard Caporaso standing under the bomb bay of a restored B-17 on tour with the Collings Foundation at Monmouth Executive Airport, Wall, NJ Sept. 2011. Photo: Mary V. Danielsen.

Photos of Gerard Caporaso under the wing of a restored B-17 on tour with the Collings Foundation at Monmouth Executive Airport, Wall, NJ Sept. 2011. Photo: Mary V. Danielsen

Photo of (from left) Robert Caporaso, Gerard Caporaso, Brigid O'Donnell and Steven Caporaso during a reunion with O'Donnell on November 5, 2012. Photo: Mary V. Danielsen

Photo of Gerard Caporaso holding military patches and pins. 2012. Photo: Mary V. Danielsen

Photo of hat with dog tags and U.S. Army Air Force pins. Photo: Mary V. Danielsen

Photo of U.S. Army Air Force flight jacket with dog tags, pins, sergeant stripes and Eighth Air Force patch. Photo: Mary V. Danielsen

Photo of Gerard Caporaso's hand holding his U.S. Army Air Force flight jacket with dog tags and pins. Photo: Mary V. Danielsen

Decorations & Citations. Photo of Gerard Caporaso's hand holding his U.S. Army Air Force dog tags and P-38 over his flight jacket. Photo: Mary V. Danielsen

Photo of wings. Photo: Mary V. Danielsen

Medals and citations photo collage. U.S. Army Air Force medals, pins, honors and dog tags given to Gerard Caporaso. Photo: Mary V. Danielsen

Photos of Honorable Discharge. Caporaso family archives

FROM THE TOP TURRET

Photo of Gerard Caporaso sitting in his living room holding his framed U.S. Army Air Force medals and citations with World War II memorabilia on the table. August 2012. Photo: Mary V. Danielsen

Wings of Freedom Tour with the Collings Foundation of Stow, Mass at the Morristown Airport, Morristown, New Jersey. August 2012. One of Gerard Caporaso's wishes was to fly again in a restored B-17. The family had twice before viewed the plane on tour in New York and New Jersey. On August 24, 2012, a perfectly clear summer day, he went on a hour-long flight over Morris County, New Jersey with his sons Steve and Bob and co-author Mary Danielsen. Ironically, the day before the flight the B-17 flew over his home in Summit, buzzing him once again. The following five photos are from that flight. Interior photos of Gerard Caporaso and plane in flight: Mary V. Danielsen. Two photo of B-17 on takeoff, taken from the ground: Charles Salin.

Photo of co-author Mary Danielsen. Photo: Jack Elberson, Elberson Photography

Mary V. Danielsen is a professional personal historian and public relations consultant. Four generations of her family have served our country in the United States military. A graduate of Rowan University, she began her career in journalism and has worked in communications for 20 years. She owns a mobile personal historian and archiving business, helping families preserve their history. A writer and photographer, Mary approaches every assignment with the philosophy that everyone has a story to tell. Preserved memories are the greatest gift we can leave the next generations. She is currently researching the art history of her great grandfather, Fidardo Landi, and working on a book about motherhood of a large family. This is her first published military memoir. Her website is www.documentedlegacy.com.

www.ingramcontent.com/pod-product-compliance
Lightning Source LLC
Chambersburg PA
CBHW041152230426
43673CB00036B/504